CHARLES VANCE

Ethical Hacking Volume 4

Enumeration Techniques: Tools for Network Recon

Powered by chatGPT

First edition

This book was professionally typeset on Reedsy.
Find out more at reedsy.com

Contents

Preface

As technology continues to advance, cybersecurity threats have become increasingly prevalent, sophisticated, and damaging. In this fast-paced and ever-changing landscape, it is essential to stay informed about the latest cybersecurity concepts, tools, and techniques.

This book, "Ethical Hacking - Volume 4: Enumeration Techniques," is the fourth volume in a series of comprehensive guides aimed at providing readers with a deeper understanding of cybersecurity and preparing them for the EC-Council CEF (Certified Encryption Specialist) exam.

In this volume, we focus on enumeration techniques, which are fundamental to network reconnaissance. We explore various enumeration tools and techniques, including SNMP enumeration, LDAP enumeration, DNS enumeration, and SMTP enumeration. The book provides practical examples and exercises to help readers understand how enumeration techniques can be applied in an ethical hacking context.

As the world becomes more connected, the need for effective network reconnaissance has become critical to identifying vulnerabilities and improving network security. This volume provides readers with a comprehensive understanding of how to effectively enumerate networks and devices, including detecting and responding to enumeration attempts, vulnerabilities, and cyberattacks.

We hope that this book will serve as an invaluable resource for cybersecurity professionals, network administrators, and anyone interested in improving their network reconnaissance skills. Our goal is to provide a practical and accessible guide that will help readers achieve the EC-Council CEF certification and enhance their cybersecurity knowledge.

We would like to express our appreciation to our readers for choosing this book, and we hope that it will exceed your expectations. We invite you to join us on this exciting journey into the world of ethical hacking and network security.

1

Introduction

In the context of cybersecurity, enumeration refers to the process of gathering information about a network, system, or application. This information can include details such as usernames, groups, shares, network resources, and services. Enumeration is typically used as part of the reconnaissance phase of an attack to gain a better understanding of the target and identify potential vulnerabilities. However, enumeration can also be used as a defensive technique to identify and mitigate security risks.

The purpose of enumeration in cybersecurity is to gather information about a target network, system, or application. This information can be used to identify potential vulnerabilities, weaknesses, or security gaps that can be exploited by attackers. By enumerating a target, a hacker can obtain a comprehensive understanding of the target's network topology, operating systems, software applications, and services. This information can then be used to launch further attacks, such as privilege escalation, password cracking, and other techniques to gain unauthorized access. Enumeration is also a critical component of ethical hacking, as it helps security professionals identify and remediate vulnerabilities before they can be exploited by malicious actors. By enumerating a network or system, security professionals can identify potential attack vectors and take appropriate measures to prevent or mitigate security risks.

Types of Enumeration

There are several types of enumeration techniques that can be used in cybersecurity. Some common types of enumeration include:

1. User Enumeration: This involves identifying valid usernames or user accounts on a target system or network. Attackers can use this information to launch further attacks, such as brute-force password cracking or social engineering attacks.

2. Network Enumeration: This involves identifying network resources, such as IP addresses, open ports, and running services. This information can be used to map out a network's topology and identify potential attack vectors.

3. Operating System (OS) Enumeration: This involves identifying the operating system used by a target system or network. This information can be used to identify vulnerabilities specific to that OS and launch attacks that exploit these weaknesses.

4. Service Enumeration: This involves identifying the services and applications running on a target system or network. This information can be used to identify vulnerabilities in specific services or applications and launch targeted attacks.

5. File and Share Enumeration: This involves identifying files and shares that are accessible on a target system or network. This information can be used to steal sensitive data, such as financial records or intellectual property.

6. LDAP Enumeration: This involves identifying user and group accounts within an LDAP directory. This information can be used to gain access to sensitive information or launch further attacks, such as password cracking.

7. DNS Enumeration: This involves identifying domain names and their associated IP addresses. This information can be used to map out a network's topology and identify potential attack vectors.

User Enumeration

User Enumeration is a type of enumeration technique used in cybersecurity to identify valid usernames or user accounts on a target system or network. Attackers can use this information to launch further attacks, such as brute-force password cracking or social engineering attacks.

There are various ways to perform user enumeration, including:

1. Usernames: Attackers can try common usernames, such as "admin," "root," or "guest," and other variations to see which usernames are valid on the target system or network.
2. Login Forms: Attackers can try to login to the target system or network using a list of usernames and a password list to identify which accounts are valid. This is known as brute-force password cracking.
3. Error Messages: Attackers can use error messages from login or authentication attempts to identify valid usernames.
4. Directory Services: Attackers can query directory services, such as LDAP, to obtain a list of user accounts on the target network.
5. Social Engineering: Attackers can also use social engineering techniques to obtain valid usernames or login credentials from employees or other users with access to the target system or network.

User enumeration is a critical step for attackers looking to gain unauthorized access to a system or network. It is also an important step for security professionals looking to identify and remediate vulnerabilities before they can be exploited. By understanding how user enumeration works, cybersecurity professionals can take steps to protect their systems and networks from these types of attacks.

Network Enumeration

Network Enumeration is a type of enumeration technique used in cybersecurity to identify network resources such as IP addresses, open ports, and running services on a target system or network. The purpose of network enumeration is to map out the target's network topology, identify potential attack vectors, and discover vulnerabilities that can be exploited.

There are various tools and techniques used for network enumeration, including:

1. Port Scanning: Port scanning is a technique that involves scanning a target system or network to identify open ports and the services running on those ports. Attackers can use this information to identify vulnerabilities in specific services or applications.

2. Banner Grabbing: Banner grabbing involves connecting to open ports and retrieving the banner or message that the server sends back. This banner can provide information about the operating system, software version, and other details that can be used to identify vulnerabilities.

3. Network Mapping: Network mapping involves identifying the devices, operating systems, and applications running on a target network. This information can be used to map out the network topology and identify potential attack vectors.

4. SNMP Enumeration: SNMP enumeration involves querying SNMP-enabled devices, such as routers and switches, to retrieve information about the device and the network topology.

5. DNS Enumeration: DNS enumeration involves querying DNS servers to identify domain names and their associated IP addresses. This information can be used to map out a network's topology and identify potential attack vectors.

Network enumeration is a critical step in the reconnaissance phase of an attack. It can help attackers identify potential vulnerabilities and launch targeted attacks that exploit these weaknesses. It is also an important step for security professionals looking to identify and remediate vulnerabilities before they can be exploited. By understanding how network enumeration works, cybersecurity professionals can take steps to protect their systems and networks from these types of attacks.

Operating System (OS) Enumeration

Operating System (OS) Enumeration is a type of enumeration technique used in cybersecurity to identify the operating system used by a target system or network. This information can be used to identify vulnerabilities specific to that OS and launch attacks that exploit these weaknesses.

There are various tools and techniques used for OS enumeration, including:

1. Passive OS Fingerprinting: Passive OS fingerprinting involves analyzing network traffic to identify patterns and characteristics that are unique to a particular operating system.
2. Active OS Fingerprinting: Active OS fingerprinting involves sending probes to the target system or network to elicit responses that can be used to identify the operating system.
3. Banner Grabbing: Banner grabbing can also be used for OS enumeration. It involves connecting to open ports and retrieving the banner or message that the server sends back. This banner can provide information about the operating system and other details that can be used to identify vulnerabilities.
4. Remote Operating System Detection: Remote OS detection involves using remote services to determine the operating system running on a target system or network. For example, attackers can use tools like Nmap to perform remote OS detection.

OS enumeration is a critical step in the reconnaissance phase of an attack. It can help attackers identify potential vulnerabilities and launch targeted attacks that exploit these weaknesses. It is also an important step for security professionals looking to identify and remediate vulnerabilities before they can be exploited. By understanding how OS enumeration works, cybersecurity professionals can take steps to protect their systems and networks from these types of attacks.

Service Enumeration

Service Enumeration is a type of enumeration technique used in cybersecurity to identify the services and applications running on a target system or network. This information can be used to identify vulnerabilities in specific services or applications and launch targeted attacks.

There are various tools and techniques used for service enumeration, including:

1. Port Scanning: Port scanning can be used to identify open ports and the services running on those ports. This information can be used to identify potential vulnerabilities and launch targeted attacks.
2. Banner Grabbing: Banner grabbing can also be used for service enumeration. It involves connecting to open ports and retrieving the banner or message that the server sends back. This banner can provide information about the service or application and other details that can be used to identify vulnerabilities.
3. Network Mapping: Network mapping can be used to identify the devices, operating systems, and applications running on a target network. This information can be used to map out the network topology and identify potential attack vectors.
4. SNMP Enumeration: SNMP enumeration can be used to retrieve information about the services and applications running on SNMP-enabled devices, such as routers and switches.
5. Web Application Enumeration: Web application enumeration involves identifying web applications running on a target system or network. This information can be used to identify potential vulnerabilities and launch targeted attacks.

Service enumeration is a critical step in the reconnaissance phase of an attack. It can help attackers identify potential vulnerabilities and launch targeted attacks that exploit these weaknesses. It is also an important step for security professionals looking to identify and remediate vulnerabilities before they can be exploited. By understanding how service enumeration works, cybersecurity professionals can take steps to protect their systems and networks from these types of attacks.

File and Share Enumeration

File and Share Enumeration is a type of enumeration technique used in cybersecurity to identify files and shares that are accessible on a target system or network. This information can be used to steal sensitive data, such as financial records or intellectual property.

There are various tools and techniques used for file and share enumeration, including:

1. Network Scanning: Network scanning can be used to identify file shares that are accessible on a target system or network. This information can be used to identify potential vulnerabilities and launch targeted attacks.
2. Directory Traversal: Directory traversal involves navigating through a file system to identify directories and files that are accessible. Attackers can use this technique to steal sensitive data, such as financial records or intellectual property.
3. SMB Enumeration: SMB enumeration involves querying a target system or network to retrieve information about SMB shares. This information can be used to identify potential vulnerabilities and launch targeted attacks.
4. FTP Enumeration: FTP enumeration involves querying a target system or network to retrieve information about FTP servers and the files accessible on those servers. This information can be used to steal sensitive data or launch targeted attacks.

File and share enumeration is a critical step in the reconnaissance phase of an attack. It can help attackers identify potential vulnerabilities and launch targeted attacks that exploit these weaknesses. It is also an important step for security professionals looking to identify and remediate vulnerabilities before they can be exploited. By understanding how file and share enumeration works, cybersecurity professionals can take steps to protect their systems and networks from these types of attacks.

LDAP Enumeration

LDAP (Lightweight Directory Access Protocol) Enumeration is a type of enumeration technique used in cybersecurity to identify user and group accounts within an LDAP directory. This information can be used to gain access to sensitive information or launch further attacks, such as password cracking.

There are various tools and techniques used for LDAP enumeration, including:

1. LDAP Queries: LDAP queries can be used to retrieve information about user and group accounts within an LDAP directory. Attackers can use this information to identify potential vulnerabilities and launch targeted attacks.
2. Directory Traversal: Directory traversal involves navigating through an LDAP directory to identify user and group accounts that are accessible. Attackers can use this technique to gain access to sensitive information or launch further attacks.
3. Password Spraying: Password spraying involves attempting to log in to multiple user accounts using a list of commonly used passwords. Attackers can use this technique to gain access to user accounts with weak passwords.
4. Social Engineering: Social engineering techniques can be used to obtain login credentials or other sensitive information from users with access to the LDAP directory.

LDAP enumeration is a critical step in the reconnaissance phase of an attack. It can help attackers identify potential vulnerabilities and launch targeted attacks that exploit these weaknesses. It is also an important step for security professionals looking to identify and remediate vulnerabilities before they can be exploited. By understanding how LDAP enumeration works, cybersecurity professionals can take steps to protect their systems and networks from these types of attacks.

DNS Enumeration

DNS (Domain Name System) Enumeration is a type of enumeration technique used in cybersecurity to identify domain names and their associated IP addresses. This information can be used to map out a network's topology and identify potential attack vectors.

There are various tools and techniques used for DNS enumeration, including:

1. Zone Transfers: Zone transfers can be used to transfer a copy of a DNS server's zone file to another server. This information can be used to identify domain names and IP addresses that are associated with a target system or network.
2. DNS Queries: DNS queries can be used to retrieve information about domain names and their associated IP addresses. Attackers can use this information to map out a network's topology and identify potential attack vectors.
3. Reverse DNS Lookup: Reverse DNS lookup involves querying a DNS server to retrieve the domain name associated with an IP address. This information can be used to identify potential attack vectors and launch targeted attacks.

DNS enumeration is a critical step in the reconnaissance phase of an attack. It can help attackers identify potential vulnerabilities and launch targeted attacks that exploit these weaknesses. It is also an important step for security professionals looking to identify and remediate vulnerabilities before they can be exploited. By understanding how DNS enumeration works, cybersecurity professionals can take steps to protect their systems and networks from these types of attacks.

Discussion

Enumeration is a crucial process in cybersecurity that involves collecting information about a target system or network to identify potential vulnerabilities that can be exploited. This process can involve gathering data such as usernames, IP addresses, open ports, and services. The main goal of enumeration is to obtain as much information as possible about a target system or network, so that vulnerabilities can be identified and addressed before they are exploited by attackers.

The different types of enumeration techniques used in cybersecurity include User Enumeration, Network Enumeration, Operating System (OS) Enumeration, Service Enumeration, File and Share Enumeration, and LDAP Enumeration, and DNS Enumeration. Each of these techniques provides a unique way to gather information about a target system or network.

User Enumeration, for example, is used to identify valid usernames or user accounts on a target system or network. Network Enumeration is used to identify network resources such as IP addresses, open ports, and running services on a target system or network. OS Enumeration is used to identify the operating system used by a target system or network. Service Enumeration is used to identify the services and applications running on a target system or network. File and Share Enumeration is used to identify files and shares that are accessible on a target system or network. LDAP Enumeration is used to identify user and group accounts within an LDAP directory, and DNS Enumeration is used to identify domain names and their associated IP addresses.

Overall, enumeration is important in cybersecurity because it helps identify potential vulnerabilities and attack vectors that can be exploited by attackers. By understanding the different types of enumeration techniques, security professionals can take steps to protect their systems and networks from these types of attacks. This process is critical for maintaining the integrity and security of systems and networks, and it is an essential part of any effective cybersecurity strategy.

Quiz

1. What is enumeration in cybersecurity?
2. What are the types of enumeration?
3. What is User Enumeration? What is Network Enumeration?
4. What is OS Enumeration?
5. What is Service Enumeration?
6. What is File and Share Enumeration?
7. What is LDAP Enumeration?
8. Why is enumeration important in cybersecurity?
9. What is DNS Enumeration?
10. Why is enumeration important in cybersecurity?

2

NetBIOS Enumeration

NetBIOS (Network Basic Input/Output System) Enumeration is a type of enumeration technique used in cybersecurity to identify NetBIOS services running on a target system or network. NetBIOS is an application programming interface (API) used for communication between applications running on a local area network (LAN).

NetBIOS enumeration involves identifying NetBIOS names, which are unique identifiers used to identify resources on a network. NetBIOS names can be used to identify file shares, printers, and other resources that are accessible on a target system or network.

There are various tools and techniques used for NetBIOS enumeration, including NBTScan, NetBIOS Name Service (NBNS), and Null Sessions. NBTScan is a command-line tool used for NetBIOS enumeration. It scans a target system or network and identifies NetBIOS services running on that network. NBNS is a protocol used by NetBIOS to translate NetBIOS names to IP addresses. Attackers can use NBNS to identify NetBIOS names associated with a target system or network. Null sessions can be used to connect to a NetBIOS service without requiring authentication. Attackers can use null sessions to retrieve information about NetBIOS shares and user accounts.

NetBIOS enumeration is a critical step in the reconnaissance phase of an attack. It can help attackers identify potential vulnerabilities and launch targeted attacks that exploit these weaknesses. It is also an important step for security professionals looking to identify and remediate vulnerabilities before they can be exploited. By understanding how NetBIOS enumeration works, cybersecurity professionals can take steps to protect their systems and networks from these types of attacks.

Tools for NetBios Enumeration

There are several tools available for NetBIOS enumeration. Here are a few examples:

1. NBTScan: NBTScan is a command-line tool used for NetBIOS enumeration. It can be downloaded from the following location: **http://www.inet cat.org/software/nbtscan.html**
2. NetBIOS Enumerator: NetBIOS Enumerator is a graphical user interface (GUI) tool used for NetBIOS enumeration. It can be downloaded from the following location: **https://sourceforge.net/projects/netbiosenum/**
3. SuperScan: SuperScan is a network scanner that can be used for NetBIOS enumeration. It can be downloaded from the following location: **http://www.mcafee.com/us/downloads/free-tools/superscan.aspx**
4. SoftPerfect Network Scanner: SoftPerfect Network Scanner is a multi-threaded IP, NetBIOS, and SNMP scanner. It can be downloaded from the following location: **https://www.softperfect.com/products/networksc anner/**

Note that while these tools can be used for legitimate purposes, they can also be used for malicious activities. It is important to only use them for ethical hacking or other legitimate purposes, and to ensure that all activities are in compliance with applicable laws and regulations.

NBTScan

NBTScan is a command-line tool used for NetBIOS enumeration. It is designed to scan a target system or network and identify NetBIOS services running on that network. Here are the instructions for using NBTScan:

1. Download and install NBTScan: NBTScan can be downloaded from the following location: **http://www.inetcat.org/software/nbtscan.html**. Once downloaded, extract the contents of the file to a folder on your local system.
2. Open a command prompt: To open a command prompt, click the Start menu and type "cmd" in the search box. Then, select "Command Prompt" from the list of results.
3. Navigate to the folder containing NBTScan: Use the "cd" command to navigate to the folder where you extracted the NBTScan files. For example, if you extracted the files to a folder named "NBTScan" on your desktop, you would use the following command: "cd C:\Users<your_username>\Desktop\NBTScan"
4. Run NBTScan: To run NBTScan, use the following command: "nbtscan <target_ip_address>". For example, if you want to scan the IP address 192.168.1.100, you would use the following command: "nbtscan 192.168.1.100".
5. View the results: Once the scan is complete, the results will be displayed in the command prompt window. The output will include the IP address, NetBIOS name, and MAC address of any systems or resources found on the target network.

NBTScan can also be used with various command-line options, such as "-v" for verbose output and "-h" for help. For more information on using NBTScan, consult the tool's documentation or visit the author's website.

NetBIOS Enumerator

NetBIOS Enumerator is a graphical user interface (GUI) tool used for NetBIOS enumeration. It is designed to scan a target system or network and identify NetBIOS services running on that network. Here are the instructions for using NetBIOS Enumerator:

1. Download and install NetBIOS Enumerator: NetBIOS Enumerator can be downloaded from the following location: **https://sourceforge.net/ projects/netbiosenum/**. Once downloaded, install the tool on your local system.
2. Launch NetBIOS Enumerator: Once installed, launch NetBIOS Enumerator by double-clicking the program icon on your desktop.
3. Enter the target IP address: In the "Target IP Address" field, enter the IP address of the system or network you wish to scan.
4. Select the scanning options: NetBIOS Enumerator offers several scanning options, such as scanning for shares, users, groups, and more. Select the desired options from the list of checkboxes.
5. Click the "Scan" button: Once you have selected your scanning options, click the "Scan" button to initiate the scan.
6. View the results: Once the scan is complete, the results will be displayed in the program window. The output will include the NetBIOS name, IP address, and MAC address of any systems or resources found on the target network.

NetBIOS Enumerator also offers several advanced features, such as the ability to export scan results to a CSV file and the ability to run custom scripts during the scanning process. For more information on using NetBIOS Enumerator, consult the tool's documentation or visit the author's website.

SuperScan

SuperScan is a network scanner that can be used for NetBIOS enumeration. It is designed to scan a target system or network and identify various services, including NetBIOS services, running on that network. Here are the instructions for using SuperScan:

1. Download and install SuperScan: SuperScan can be downloaded from the following location: **http://www.mcafee.com/us/downloads/free-tools/superscan.aspx**. Once downloaded, install the tool on your local system.
2. Launch SuperScan: Once installed, launch SuperScan by double-clicking the program icon on your desktop.
3. Configure the scan settings: In the SuperScan main window, click the "Profiles" button to create a new profile. Enter a name for the profile and select the scan type as "NetBIOS." Then, enter the target IP address or range of addresses you wish to scan.
4. Customize the scan options: SuperScan offers various scan options, such as selecting specific ports to scan, setting timeouts, and enabling/disabling certain scan types. Customize the scan options as per your requirements.
5. Initiate the scan: Once you have configured the scan settings and options, click the "Start" button to initiate the scan.
6. View the results: Once the scan is complete, the results will be displayed in the program window. The output will include the NetBIOS name, IP address, and MAC address of any systems or resources found on the target network.

SuperScan also offers several advanced features, such as the ability to export scan results to a CSV file and the ability to customize scan scripts. For more information on using SuperScan, consult the tool's documentation or visit the author's website.

SoftPerfect Network Scanner

SoftPerfect Network Scanner is a multi-threaded IP, NetBIOS, and SNMP scanner. It is designed to scan a target system or network and identify various services, including NetBIOS services, running on that network. Here are the instructions for using SoftPerfect Network Scanner:

1. Download and install SoftPerfect Network Scanner: SoftPerfect Network Scanner can be downloaded from the following location: **https://www.softperfect.com/products/networkscanner/**. Once downloaded, install the tool on your local system.
2. Launch SoftPerfect Network Scanner: Once installed, launch SoftPerfect Network Scanner by double-clicking the program icon on your desktop.
3. Configure the scan settings: In the SoftPerfect Network Scanner main window, click the "New Scan" button to create a new scan profile. Enter a name for the profile and select the scan type as "NetBIOS." Then, enter the target IP address or range of addresses you wish to scan.
4. Customize the scan options: SoftPerfect Network Scanner offers various scan options, such as selecting specific ports to scan, setting timeouts, and enabling/disabling certain scan types. Customize the scan options as per your requirements.
5. Initiate the scan: Once you have configured the scan settings and options, click the "Start Scanning" button to initiate the scan.
6. View the results: Once the scan is complete, the results will be displayed in the program window. The output will include the NetBIOS name, IP address, and MAC address of any systems or resources found on the target network.

SoftPerfect Network Scanner also offers several advanced features, such as the ability to export scan results to a CSV file, and the ability to customize scan scripts. For more information on using SoftPerfect Network Scanner, consult the tool's documentation or visit the author's website.

Identified Vulnerabilities

NetBIOS enumeration can help identify various vulnerabilities that can be exploited by attackers to gain unauthorized access to systems or networks. Here are some common vulnerabilities that can be identified through NetBIOS enumeration:

1. Weak or default passwords: NetBIOS enumeration can identify accounts with weak or default passwords, which can be easily guessed or cracked by attackers.
2. Misconfigured shares: NetBIOS enumeration can identify shared resources that have been misconfigured and are accessible to unauthorized users.
3. Unpatched systems: NetBIOS enumeration can identify systems that are running outdated or unpatched software, making them vulnerable to known exploits.
4. Open ports: NetBIOS enumeration can identify open ports that can be used by attackers to gain unauthorized access to systems or networks.
5. Missing security updates: NetBIOS enumeration can identify missing security updates, such as missing patches or updates for antivirus software, that can leave systems vulnerable to attacks.
6. Weak encryption: NetBIOS enumeration can identify systems that are using weak encryption methods or that are not using encryption at all, making them vulnerable to eavesdropping attacks.

It is important to note that while NetBIOS enumeration can help identify these vulnerabilities, it should only be used for ethical hacking or other legitimate purposes, and all activities should be in compliance with applicable laws and regulations.

Countermeasures

There are several countermeasures that organizations can take to prevent or mitigate the risks associated with NetBIOS enumeration. Here are some of the most effective countermeasures:

1. Disable NetBIOS: One of the most effective countermeasures is to disable NetBIOS over TCP/IP. This can be done by disabling the NetBIOS interface in network settings or by blocking the NetBIOS ports.
2. Use firewalls: Firewalls can be used to block unauthorized access to NetBIOS services and to block NetBIOS traffic from entering or leaving the network.
3. Use strong passwords: Organizations should ensure that all user accounts have strong passwords that are difficult to guess or crack. Password policies should require users to change their passwords regularly and should enforce password complexity requirements.
4. Patch systems and software: Organizations should ensure that all systems and software are up-to-date with the latest security patches and updates to prevent known vulnerabilities from being exploited.
5. Implement access controls: Access controls can be used to limit the number of users who have access to sensitive resources on the network, such as shared folders.
6. Use encryption: Organizations should use strong encryption methods, such as SSL/TLS, to protect sensitive data in transit and at rest.
7. Conduct regular security assessments: Regular security assessments, such as vulnerability scans and penetration testing, can help identify vulnerabilities before they can be exploited by attackers.

By implementing these countermeasures, organizations can significantly reduce the risk of NetBIOS enumeration and other types of cyberattacks.

Discussion

NetBIOS enumeration is a process of collecting information about NetBIOS services running on a target system or network. It is considered a security risk because it can reveal information that can be used by attackers to gain unauthorized access to systems or networks. Tools used for NetBIOS enumeration include NBTScan, NetBIOS Enumerator, and SoftPerfect Network Scanner. Common vulnerabilities that can be identified through NetBIOS enumeration include weak passwords, misconfigured shares, unpatched systems, open ports, missing security updates, and weak encryption.

To protect against NetBIOS enumeration, organizations can disable NetBIOS, use firewalls, implement access controls, use encryption, and conduct regular security assessments. NetBIOS is a protocol used for communicating with other devices on a network, while NetBIOS over TCP/IP is a variant of NetBIOS that is used over TCP/IP networks. The purpose of the NetBIOS name service (NBNS) is to provide a way for NetBIOS names to be resolved to IP addresses on a network. Some NetBIOS ports that are commonly used include UDP port 137 (NetBIOS name service), UDP port 138 (NetBIOS datagram service), and TCP port 139 (NetBIOS session service).

NetBIOS is different from SMB (Server Message Block), which is a protocol used for sharing files, printers, and other resources on a network. The potential impact of a successful NetBIOS enumeration attack can range from unauthorized access to sensitive data and resources, to the compromise of entire networks or systems. Therefore, it is important to take proactive measures to protect against NetBIOS enumeration, including implementing strong access controls, using encryption, and keeping systems and software up-to-date with the latest security patches and updates.

Quiz

1. What is NetBIOS enumeration?
2. Why is NetBIOS enumeration considered a security risk?
3. What are some tools used for NetBIOS enumeration?

4. What are some common vulnerabilities that can be identified through NetBIOS enumeration?
5. How can organizations protect against NetBIOS enumeration?
6. What is the difference between NetBIOS and NetBIOS over TCP/IP?
7. What is the purpose of the NetBIOS name service (NBNS)?
8. What are some NetBIOS ports that are commonly used?
9. What is the difference between NetBIOS and SMB?
10. What is the potential impact of a successful NetBIOS enumeration attack?

3

SNMP Enumeration

SNMP enumeration is the process of collecting information about devices on a network that use the Simple Network Management Protocol (SNMP). SNMP is a protocol that is commonly used to manage and monitor devices on a network, such as routers, switches, and servers. SNMP enumeration can help identify potential vulnerabilities in network devices and can be used to gather information about the configuration of devices on the network.

SNMP enumeration typically involves sending SNMP queries to a target device using a tool such as SNMPWalk or SNMPUtil. These queries can be used to retrieve information about the device, such as the device name, system uptime, installed software and firmware versions, network interfaces, and configuration details. SNMP enumeration can also be used to retrieve information about other devices on the network that are managed by the target device.

SNMP enumeration can be used for both legitimate and malicious purposes. For example, network administrators can use SNMP enumeration to gather information about devices on their network and to identify potential security risks. However, attackers can also use SNMP enumeration to gather information about the network and to identify potential vulnerabilities that can be exploited.

To protect against SNMP enumeration attacks, organizations can implement strong access controls, restrict SNMP access to authorized users and devices, and use encryption to protect SNMP traffic. Organizations should also keep their network devices up-to-date with the latest security patches and updates, and regularly conduct security assessments to identify potential vulnerabilities.

Tools used for SNMP Enumeration

Here are some commonly used tools for SNMP enumeration along with their download links:

1. SNMPWalk: SNMPWalk is a command-line tool that can be used to query SNMP-enabled devices and retrieve information about the device's configuration. It can be downloaded from the following link: **https://sou rceforge.net/projects/net-snmp/files/net-snmp%20binaries/5.7.3/**

2. SNMPUtil: SNMPUtil is another command-line tool that can be used to query SNMP-enabled devices and retrieve information about the device's configuration. It can be downloaded from the following link: **https://ww w.snmpsoft.com/downloads/**

3. SolarWinds Network Performance Monitor: SolarWinds Network Performance Monitor is a network monitoring tool that includes SNMP enumeration capabilities. It can be used to monitor SNMP-enabled devices and to gather information about the device's configuration. A free trial can be downloaded from the following link: **https://www.solar winds.com/network-performance-monitor/registration**

4. Paessler PRTG Network Monitor: Paessler PRTG Network Monitor is another network monitoring tool that includes SNMP enumeration capabilities. It can be used to monitor SNMP-enabled devices and to gather information about the device's configuration. A free trial can be downloaded from the following link: **https://www.paessler.com/prtg/ download**

5. Net-SNMP: Net-SNMP is a suite of SNMP tools that includes a command-line tool for querying SNMP-enabled devices and retrieving information about the device's configuration. It can be downloaded from the following

link: **https://sourceforge.net/projects/net-snmp/files/net-snmp%2 obinaries/5.7.3/**

It is important to note that while these tools can be used for legitimate purposes, they can also be used by attackers to gather information about network devices and to identify potential vulnerabilities. Therefore, it is important to use these tools responsibly and to ensure that all activities are in compliance with applicable laws and regulations.

SNMPWalk

SNMPWalk is a command-line tool that is used for SNMP enumeration. It is typically used to retrieve information about SNMP-enabled devices on a network. SNMPWalk works by sending SNMP queries to a target device and retrieving information about the device's configuration.

To use SNMPWalk, follow these instructions:

Download and install SNMPWalk on your system. You can download it from the following link: **https://sourceforge.net/projects/net-snmp/files/net-snmp%20binaries/5.7.3/**

Open a command prompt on your system.

Type the following command: snmpwalk -c <community_string> -v <version> <IP_address>

The community string is a password-like string that is used to authenticate SNMP messages. The version is the SNMP version that is being used, such as SNMPv1, SNMPv2c, or SNMPv3. The IP address is the IP address of the target device.

Press Enter.

SNMPWalk will then send SNMP queries to the target device and retrieve information about the device's configuration. The information retrieved may include the device name, system uptime, installed software and firmware versions, network interfaces, and configuration details.

It is important to note that SNMPWalk can be used for both legitimate and malicious purposes. Therefore, it is important to use SNMPWalk responsibly and to ensure that all activities are in compliance with applicable laws and regulations. It is also important to secure SNMP-enabled devices by using strong access controls, restricting SNMP access to authorized users and devices, and using encryption to protect SNMP traffic.

SNMPUtil

SNMPUtil is a command-line tool that is used for SNMP enumeration. It is typically used to retrieve information about SNMP-enabled devices on a network. SNMPUtil works by sending SNMP queries to a target device and retrieving information about the device's configuration.

To use SNMPUtil, follow these instructions:

Download and install SNMPUtil on your system. You can download it from the following link: **https://www.snmpsoft.com/downloads/**

Open a command prompt on your system.

Type the following command: snmputil -c <community_string> -v <version> <IP_address>

The community string is a password-like string that is used to authenticate SNMP messages. The version is the SNMP version that is being used, such as SNMPv1, SNMPv2c, or SNMPv3. The IP address is the IP address of the target device.

Press Enter.

SNMPUtil will then send SNMP queries to the target device and retrieve information about the device's configuration. The information retrieved may include the device name, system uptime, installed software and firmware versions, network interfaces, and configuration details.

It is important to note that SNMPUtil can be used for both legitimate and malicious purposes. Therefore, it is important to use SNMPUtil responsibly and to ensure that all activities are in compliance with applicable laws and regulations. It is also important to secure SNMP-enabled devices by using strong access controls, restricting SNMP access to authorized users and devices, and using encryption to protect SNMP traffic.

SolarWinds Network Performance Monitor

SolarWinds Network Performance Monitor is a network monitoring tool that includes SNMP enumeration capabilities. It can be used to monitor SNMP-enabled devices and to gather information about the device's configuration. SolarWinds Network Performance Monitor is a paid tool, but a free trial can be downloaded from the following link: **https://www.solarwinds.com/network-performance-monitor/registration**

To use SolarWinds Network Performance Monitor, follow these instructions:

1. Download and install SolarWinds Network Performance Monitor on your system.
2. Open SolarWinds Network Performance Monitor.
3. Add the target device to the tool by specifying its IP address or hostname.
4. Select the device from the list of monitored devices.
5. SolarWinds Network Performance Monitor will then begin monitoring the device and gathering information about its configuration.

The information retrieved by SolarWinds Network Performance Monitor may include the device name, system uptime, installed software and firmware versions, network interfaces, and configuration details.

It is important to note that SolarWinds Network Performance Monitor can be used for both legitimate and malicious purposes. Therefore, it is important to use SolarWinds Network Performance Monitor responsibly and to ensure that all activities are in compliance with applicable laws and regulations. It is also important to secure SNMP-enabled devices by using strong access controls, restricting SNMP access to authorized users and devices, and using encryption to protect SNMP traffic.

Paessler PRTG Network Monitor

Paessler PRTG Network Monitor is another network monitoring tool that includes SNMP enumeration capabilities. It can be used to monitor SNMP-enabled devices and to gather information about the device's configuration. Paessler PRTG Network Monitor is a paid tool, but a free trial can be downloaded from the following link: **https://www.paessler.com/prtg/download**

To use Paessler PRTG Network Monitor, follow these instructions:

1. Download and install Paessler PRTG Network Monitor on your system.
2. Open Paessler PRTG Network Monitor.
3. Add the target device to the tool by specifying its IP address or hostname.
4. Configure the SNMP settings for the device, such as the community string and SNMP version.
5. Paessler PRTG Network Monitor will then begin monitoring the device and gathering information about its configuration.

The information retrieved by Paessler PRTG Network Monitor may include the device name, system uptime, installed software and firmware versions, network interfaces, and configuration details.

It is important to note that Paessler PRTG Network Monitor can be used for both legitimate and malicious purposes. Therefore, it is important to use Paessler PRTG Network Monitor responsibly and to ensure that all activities are in compliance with applicable laws and regulations. It is also important to secure SNMP-enabled devices by using strong access controls, restricting SNMP access to authorized users and devices, and using encryption to protect SNMP traffic.

Net-SNMP

Net-SNMP is a suite of SNMP tools that includes a command-line tool for querying SNMP-enabled devices and retrieving information about the device's configuration. It can be downloaded from the following link: **https://sourcef orge.net/projects/net-snmp/files/net-snmp%20binaries/5.7.3/**

To use Net-SNMP, follow these instructions:

1. Download and install Net-SNMP on your system.
2. Open a command prompt on your system.
3. Type the following command: snmpwalk -c <community_string> -v <version> <IP_address>

The community string is a password-like string that is used to authenticate SNMP messages. The version is the SNMP version that is being used, such as SNMPv1, SNMPv2c, or SNMPv3. The IP address is the IP address of the target device.

1. Press Enter.

Net-SNMP will then send SNMP queries to the target device and retrieve information about the device's configuration. The information retrieved may include the device name, system uptime, installed software and firmware versions, network interfaces, and configuration details.

It is important to note that Net-SNMP can be used for both legitimate and malicious purposes. Therefore, it is important to use Net-SNMP responsibly and to ensure that all activities are in compliance with applicable laws and regulations. It is also important to secure SNMP-enabled devices by using strong access controls, restricting SNMP access to authorized users and devices, and using encryption to protect SNMP traffic.

Vulnerabilities identified through SNMP Enumeration

SNMP Enumeration can reveal vulnerabilities in SNMP-enabled devices and their network infrastructure. Some of the vulnerabilities that can be identified through SNMP Enumeration include:

1. Weak SNMP Community Strings: SNMP Community Strings are used to authenticate SNMP messages. If weak or default community strings are used, they can be easily guessed or discovered by attackers, allowing them to gain unauthorized access to SNMP-enabled devices.
2. SNMP Version Vulnerabilities: Different versions of SNMP have different security vulnerabilities. For example, SNMPv1 and SNMPv2c use plain-text passwords that can be easily intercepted, while SNMPv3 is more secure but can still be vulnerable to certain attacks.
3. Unauthorized Access: SNMP Enumeration can reveal unauthorized SNMP access to devices. This can include access by unauthorized users, devices, or applications.
4. Configuration Vulnerabilities: SNMP Enumeration can reveal miscon-figured SNMP settings on devices, which can leave them vulnerable to attack. For example, SNMP settings may be configured to allow access from any IP address, which can allow attackers to gain unauthorized access.
5. Device Vulnerabilities: SNMP Enumeration can also reveal vulnerabilities in the devices themselves, such as outdated firmware or software, unpatched security flaws, and default or weak passwords.

It is important to note that SNMP Enumeration can be used for both legitimate and malicious purposes. Therefore, it is important to use SNMP Enumeration responsibly and to ensure that all activities are in compliance with applicable laws and regulations. It is also important to secure SNMP-enabled devices by using strong access controls, restricting SNMP access to authorized users and devices, and using encryption to protect SNMP traffic.

Countermeasures

There are several countermeasures that can be implemented to protect against SNMP Enumeration. These include:

1. Strong SNMP Community Strings: Use strong and unique community strings for SNMP-enabled devices. Avoid using default or easily guessable strings.
2. SNMP Version Control: Use the latest version of SNMP that is compatible with your devices. For example, use SNMPv3 instead of SNMPv1 or SNMPv2c.
3. Access Controls: Restrict SNMP access to authorized users and devices only. Use access control lists (ACLs) to limit SNMP access to trusted IP addresses or ranges of IP addresses.
4. Encryption: Use encryption to protect SNMP traffic from interception and eavesdropping.
5. Configuration Management: Implement strong configuration management practices to ensure that SNMP-enabled devices are properly configured and secured. This includes disabling SNMP if it is not needed, using strong passwords, and updating firmware and software regularly.
6. Network Monitoring: Use network monitoring tools to detect unauthorized SNMP activity and anomalous behavior on the network.

By implementing these countermeasures, organizations can reduce the risk of SNMP Enumeration and protect their SNMP-enabled devices and network infrastructure. It is important to regularly review and update these countermeasures to stay up-to-date with the latest security threats and vulnerabilities.

Discussion

SNMP Enumeration is the process of gathering information about SNMP-enabled devices on a network. Various tools are used for SNMP Enumeration, including SNMPWalk, SNMPUtil, SolarWinds Network Performance Monitor, Paessler PRTG Network Monitor, and Net-SNMP. SNMPWalk is a command-line tool used to retrieve SNMP information from devices. SNMPUtil is another command-line tool that is used to perform SNMP operations on devices. Solar-Winds Network Performance Monitor and Paessler PRTG Network Monitor are network monitoring tools that include SNMP Enumeration capabilities. Net-SNMP is a suite of SNMP tools that includes a command-line tool for querying SNMP-enabled devices and retrieving information about their configuration.

SNMP Enumeration can identify vulnerabilities in SNMP-enabled devices, including weak SNMP community strings, SNMP version vulnerabilities, unauthorized access, configuration vulnerabilities, and device vulnerabilities. To protect against SNMP Enumeration, countermeasures such as using strong SNMP community strings, SNMP version control, access controls, encryption, configuration management, and network monitoring can be implemented.

Securing SNMP-enabled devices is important because they can be vulnerable to attacks if they are not properly secured. Attackers can use SNMP Enumeration to gather information about a device's configuration and use that information to launch further attacks. Therefore, it is essential to implement appropriate security measures to protect SNMP-enabled devices and network infrastructure. By using strong passwords, restricting access to SNMP-enabled devices, keeping software and firmware updated, and monitoring the network for unauthorized activity, organizations can reduce the risk of SNMP Enumeration and other types of attacks.

Quiz

1. What is SNMP Enumeration?
2. What are the tools used for SNMP Enumeration?
3. What is SNMPWalk and how is it used?

4. What is SNMPUtil and how is it used?
5. What is SolarWinds Network Performance Monitor and how is it used for SNMP Enumeration?
6. What is Paessler PRTG Network Monitor and how is it used for SNMP Enumeration?
7. What is Net-SNMP and how is it used for SNMP Enumeration?
8. What are the vulnerabilities that can be identified through SNMP Enumeration?
9. What are the countermeasures that can be implemented to protect against SNMP Enumeration?
10. Why is it important to secure SNMP-enabled devices?

4

LDAP Enumeration

LDAP Enumeration is the process of querying a Lightweight Directory Access Protocol (LDAP) directory to obtain information about user and group accounts. LDAP is a protocol used for accessing and managing distributed directory information services over a network. LDAP directories are commonly used in enterprise environments to store user and group account information, such as usernames, email addresses, and group memberships.

During LDAP Enumeration, an attacker can use tools and techniques to query an LDAP directory to gather information about user and group accounts. This information can be used to identify potential targets for further attacks, such as password cracking or social engineering. LDAP Enumeration can also reveal vulnerabilities in the LDAP directory itself, such as misconfigured access controls or weak authentication methods.

LDAP Enumeration can be performed manually using command-line tools, such as ldapsearch or JXplorer, or automated tools, such as enum4linux or Nmap's LDAP NSE scripts. These tools allow an attacker to search an LDAP directory for user and group account information and obtain details about the directory structure and permissions.

LDAP Enumeration can be prevented by implementing appropriate security controls, such as using strong passwords, restricting access to LDAP directories, and using encryption to protect LDAP traffic. It is also important to regularly review and update LDAP directory access controls to ensure that they remain effective and up-to-date with the latest security threats and vulnerabilities.

In summary, LDAP Enumeration is a technique used by attackers to gather information about user and group accounts stored in an LDAP directory. Organizations can prevent LDAP Enumeration by implementing appropriate security controls and regularly reviewing and updating their LDAP directory access controls.

Tools used for LDAP Enumeration

Here is a list of tools that can be used for LDAP Enumeration, along with their download links:

1. ldapsearch: ldapsearch is a command-line tool that is included with most LDAP software distributions. It can be downloaded from the OpenLDAP website: **https://www.openldap.org/software/download/**
2. JXplorer: JXplorer is a Java-based LDAP browser that can be used to view and edit LDAP directories. It can be downloaded from the JXplorer website: **https://jxplorer.org/downloads/index.html**
3. enum4linux: enum4linux is a command-line tool that can be used to enumerate Windows and Samba hosts over an LDAP directory. It can be downloaded from the GitHub repository: **https://github.com/CiscoCXS ecurity/enum4linux**
4. Nmap: Nmap is a network mapping and port scanning tool that includes LDAP Enumeration capabilities. It can be downloaded from the Nmap website: **https://nmap.org/download.html**
5. Metasploit: Metasploit is a penetration testing framework that includes several modules for LDAP Enumeration. It can be downloaded from the Metasploit website: **https://www.metasploit.com/downloads**

It is important to note that these tools should only be used for ethical purposes, such as testing the security of LDAP directories in a controlled environment. Using these tools for malicious purposes can result in legal consequences.

ldapsearch

ldapsearch is a command-line tool that can be used to query an LDAP directory for information about user and group accounts. It is included with most LDAP software distributions, such as OpenLDAP.

To use ldapsearch, you will need to have access to an LDAP directory and know the correct server and port to connect to. You will also need to know the search base, which is the starting point for the search, and the search filter, which is the criteria used to filter the results.

Here is an example command for ldapsearch:

ldapsearch -x -H ldap://ldap.example.com -b "dc=example,dc=com" "(objectClass=person)"

This command searches for all person objects in the example.com domain. Here is a breakdown of the command:

- **-x**: Use simple authentication instead of SASL authentication.
- **-H**: Specify the LDAP server to connect to.
- **-b**: Specify the search base.
- **(objectClass=person)**: Specify the search filter. This filter searches for all objects with the objectClass attribute set to "person".

When you run the command, you should see a list of all the person objects in the example.com domain that match the search filter.

ldapsearch can be used to search for a wide range of attributes and filters, depending on the information you are trying to obtain. It is a powerful tool that can be used for both legitimate and illegitimate purposes, so it is important to use it ethically and with appropriate authorization.

JXplorer

JXplorer is a Java-based LDAP browser that can be used to view and edit LDAP directories. It is a cross-platform tool that can run on Windows, Linux, and macOS.

To use JXplorer, you will need to have access to an LDAP directory and know the correct server and port to connect to. You will also need to know the username and password for the LDAP directory, as well as any other necessary authentication parameters.

Here are the basic steps for using JXplorer:

1. Download and install JXplorer from the official website: **https://jxplore r.org/downloads/index.html**
2. Open JXplorer and click the "Connect" button in the toolbar.
3. Enter the LDAP server information, including the server name, port number, and protocol.
4. Enter the authentication information, including the username, password, and any other necessary parameters.
5. Click the "Connect" button to connect to the LDAP directory.
6. Once connected, you can browse the LDAP directory and view or edit the contents as necessary.

JXplorer allows you to view and edit a wide range of LDAP attributes, including user and group account information, as well as organizational unit and directory tree structures. It also includes a search function that allows you to search for specific objects or attributes within the LDAP directory.

JXplorer is a powerful tool that can be used for both legitimate and illegitimate purposes, so it is important to use it ethically and with appropriate authorization.

enum4linux

enum4linux is a command-line tool that can be used to enumerate Windows and Samba hosts over an LDAP directory. It is a Linux-based tool and is typically used in a penetration testing context to gather information about user and group accounts, as well as share information and password policies.
Here are the basic steps for using enum4linux:

1. Download enum4linux from the official GitHub repository: **https://gith ub.com/CiscoCXSecurity/enum4linux**
2. Extract the downloaded files to a local directory.
3. Open a terminal window and navigate to the directory where you extracted the files.
4. Run the enum4linux command, specifying the target host and any necessary authentication parameters.

Here is an example command for using enum4linux:
enum4linux -a -u user1 -p password1 192.168.1.100

This command runs a full enumeration of the target host with the IP address of 192.168.1.100, using the username "user1" and the password "password1" for authentication.
enum4linux can be used to extract a wide range of information from Windows and Samba hosts, including user and group account information, password policies, and share information. It is a powerful tool that can be used for both legitimate and illegitimate purposes, so it is important to use it ethically and with appropriate authorization.

Nmap

Nmap is a network mapping and port scanning tool that includes LDAP Enumeration capabilities. It is a cross-platform tool that can run on Windows, Linux, and macOS.

Here are the basic steps for using Nmap for LDAP Enumeration:

Download and install Nmap from the official website: **https://nmap.org/ download.html**

Open a terminal window and navigate to the directory where Nmap is installed.

Run the following command to scan for LDAP services on a target host:

nmap -sV -p 389 —script ldap-search

This command scans the target host with IP address **<target_ip>** for LDAP services on port 389, and uses the Nmap script "ldap-search" to perform the enumeration.

Review the output of the scan to see the results of the LDAP enumeration.

Nmap can be used to scan for a wide range of ports and services, and can also perform advanced scanning techniques such as OS fingerprinting and vulnerability scanning. It is a powerful tool that can be used for both legitimate and illegitimate purposes, so it is important to use it ethically and with appropriate authorization.

Metasploit

Metasploit is a penetration testing framework that includes a wide range of tools and modules for network mapping, vulnerability scanning, exploita-tion, and post-exploitation activities. It includes several modules for LDAP Enumeration.

Here are the basic steps for using Metasploit for LDAP Enumeration:

Download and install Metasploit from the official website: **https://www.met**

asploit.com/download

Open the Metasploit console and enter the following command to search for LDAP Enumeration modules:

search ldap_enum

This command lists all available LDAP Enumeration modules in Metasploit.

Select the module you want to use, such as "auxiliary/scanner/ldap/ldap_search", and enter the following command to use the module:

use auxiliary/scanner/ldap/ldap_search

Set the necessary options for the module, such as the target host and LDAP authentication information.

Run the module and review the output to see the results of the LDAP Enumeration.

Metasploit includes several other modules for LDAP Enumeration, as well as other advanced scanning and exploitation capabilities. It is a powerful tool that can be used for both legitimate and illegitimate purposes, so it is important to use it ethically and with appropriate authorization.

Vulnerabilities identified through LDAP Enumeration

LDAP Enumeration can reveal several vulnerabilities in a target system or network, including:

1. User enumeration: LDAP Enumeration can be used to enumerate valid user accounts on a target system or network, which can then be targeted for further attacks such as brute force attacks or password spraying.

2. Group enumeration: LDAP Enumeration can also reveal the groups and permissions associated with each user account, which can provide valuable information for privilege escalation attacks.

3. Password policy enumeration: LDAP Enumeration can be used to identify the password policies in use on a target system or network, which can reveal weaknesses or vulnerabilities in the password policy that can be exploited.

4. Share and resource enumeration: LDAP Enumeration can be used to identify the shares and resources available on a target system or network, which can provide information for further attacks such as lateral movement or data exfiltration.

5. Server enumeration: LDAP Enumeration can also reveal information about the servers and services in use on a target system or network, which can be used to identify vulnerabilities and attack vectors.

By revealing these vulnerabilities, LDAP Enumeration can provide valuable information for security professionals to take appropriate measures to mitigate or remediate these vulnerabilities before they can be exploited by attackers. It is important to use LDAP Enumeration tools ethically and with appropriate authorization, as they can be used for both legitimate and illegitimate purposes.

Countermeasures for LDAP Enumeration

Here are some countermeasures that can be implemented to mitigate the risk of LDAP Enumeration attacks:

1. Implement access controls: Access controls should be implemented to limit the information that can be accessed through LDAP queries. Only authorized users should be granted access to sensitive information.

2. Implement rate limiting: Rate limiting can be used to limit the number of LDAP queries that can be performed within a specific time period. This can help prevent brute force attacks and other enumeration techniques.

3. Use secure authentication: Secure authentication mechanisms such as LDAP over SSL (LDAPS) or LDAP over Transport Layer Security (LDAP-TLS) should be used to protect against man-in-the-middle attacks and other forms of eavesdropping.

4. Disable anonymous LDAP access: Anonymous LDAP access should be disabled to prevent unauthorized access to LDAP directories.

5. Implement network segmentation: Network segmentation can be used to limit the scope of LDAP queries and prevent attackers from accessing sensitive information.

6. Monitor LDAP traffic: Monitoring LDAP traffic can help identify and respond to LDAP Enumeration attacks in real-time.

7. Implement password policies: Strong password policies should be implemented to prevent brute force attacks and other password-based attacks.

8. Keep software up-to-date: Keeping LDAP server software up-to-date with the latest patches and updates can help prevent known vulnerabilities from being exploited.

By implementing these countermeasures, organizations can reduce the risk of LDAP Enumeration attacks and improve the overall security posture of their systems and networks.

Discussion

LDAP Enumeration is a critical step in the reconnaissance phase of a cybersecurity attack. Attackers can use this technique to gather information about a target system or network by querying its LDAP directory service. The tools used for LDAP Enumeration include ldapsearch, JXplorer, enum4linux, and Metasploit.

LDAP Enumeration can reveal several vulnerabilities, including user enumeration, group enumeration, password policy enumeration, share and resource enumeration, and server enumeration. Attackers can exploit these vulnerabilities to launch further attacks such as brute force attacks, password spraying, or privilege escalation attacks. To mitigate the risk of LDAP Enumeration attacks, countermeasures such as access controls, rate limiting, secure authentication, and network segmentation should be implemented.

Ldapsearch is a command-line tool used for querying LDAP directories. It can be used for LDAP Enumeration by specifying search criteria and performing queries on a target system or network. JXplorer is a graphical tool used for browsing and querying LDAP directories. It can be used for LDAP Enumeration by connecting to a target system or network and performing queries to gather information. Enum4linux is a tool used for enumerating information from Windows and Samba systems. It includes LDAP Enumeration capabilities that can be used to gather information about LDAP directories. Metasploit is a penetration testing framework that includes modules for LDAP Enumeration. It can be used to scan for LDAP services, perform queries, and gather information about a target system or network.

LDAP Enumeration is important in cybersecurity because it can help identify potential vulnerabilities and attack vectors that can be exploited by attackers. By understanding the techniques and tools used for LDAP Enumeration, security professionals can take steps to protect their systems and networks from these types of attacks. It is important to use LDAP Enumeration tools ethically and with appropriate authorization, as they can be used for both legitimate and illegitimate purposes.

Quiz

1. What is LDAP Enumeration?
2. What are the tools used for LDAP Enumeration?
3. What are the vulnerabilities identified through LDAP Enumeration?
4. How can LDAP Enumeration be used by attackers?
5. What are the countermeasures for LDAP Enumeration?
6. What is ldapsearch and how is it used for LDAP Enumeration?
7. What is JXplorer and how is it used for LDAP Enumeration?
8. What is enum4linux and how is it used for LDAP Enumeration?
9. What is Metasploit and how is it used for LDAP Enumeration?

10. Why is LDAP Enumeration important in cybersecurity?

5

NTP and NFS Enumeration

NTP and NFS Enumeration are two techniques used in the reconnaissance phase of a cybersecurity attack. NTP Enumeration is the process of gathering information about Network Time Protocol (NTP) servers, which are used for time synchronization in computer networks. NFS Enumeration is the process of gathering information about Network File System (NFS) shares, which allow users to access files and directories on remote systems as if they were on their local systems.

NTP Enumeration can reveal information such as the IP address, hostname, and version of the NTP server. This information can be used by attackers to launch further attacks such as DoS attacks, time-stamping attacks, or data modification attacks. Countermeasures for NTP Enumeration include implementing access controls, rate limiting, and secure authentication mechanisms.

NFS Enumeration can reveal information such as the shared directories and files available on a remote system. Attackers can exploit this information to gain unauthorized access to sensitive files and data. Countermeasures for NFS Enumeration include implementing access controls, limiting access to NFS shares, and using secure authentication mechanisms.

Tools used for NTP Enumeration include Nmap, which can be used to scan for open NTP ports, and ntpq, which can be used to query NTP servers. Tools used for NFS Enumeration include showmount, which can be used to list NFS shares on a remote system, and nfsstat, which can be used to display NFS statistics.

It is important to use NTP and NFS Enumeration tools ethically and with appropriate authorization, as they can be used for both legitimate and illegitimate purposes. By understanding the techniques and tools used for NTP and NFS Enumeration, security professionals can take steps to protect their systems and networks from these types of attacks.

Tools used for NTP and NFS Enumeration

here are some tools used for NTP and NFS Enumeration with brief descriptions and their download links:

NTP Enumeration:

- Nmap: Nmap is a popular network scanning tool that can be used to scan for open NTP ports. It can be downloaded from the official website: **https://nmap.org/**
- ntpq: ntpq is a command-line tool that can be used to query NTP servers and retrieve information such as the IP address, hostname, and version of the NTP server. It is included with most NTP client packages and can also be downloaded separately from the official NTP support website: **https://support.ntp.org/bin/view/Support/DocumentationNtpq**

NFS Enumeration:

- showmount: showmount is a command-line tool that can be used to list NFS shares on a remote system. It is included with most NFS client packages and can also be downloaded separately for Linux systems from the Linux man pages website: **https://linux.die.net/man/8/showmount**
- nfsstat: nfsstat is a command-line tool that can be used to display NFS statistics such as the number of requests, errors, and bytes transferred. It is included with most NFS client packages and can also be downloaded separately for Linux systems from the Linux man pages website: **https://l**

inux.die.net/man/8/nfsstat

Nmap

Nmap (Network Mapper) is a popular open-source tool used for network exploration, management, and security auditing. It can be used for a variety of purposes, including host discovery, port scanning, version detection, and vulnerability scanning. Nmap is available for Windows, Linux, and macOS operating systems and can be downloaded from the official website: **https://nmap.org/download.html**.

Here are some instructions for using Nmap:

1. Installing Nmap: Nmap can be downloaded and installed on your system from the official website or via the package manager on Linux distributions.
2. Basic Scanning: The simplest way to use Nmap is to run a basic scan with default options. To do this, open the terminal or command prompt and type the following command:

```phpCopy code
nmap <target>
```

Replace **<target>** with the IP address or hostname of the target system or network.

Port Scanning: Nmap can be used to scan for open ports on a target system or network. To do this, use the **-p** option followed by a list of port numbers or ranges. For example, to scan for open ports on port 80 and 443, use the following command:

```
cssCopy code
nmap -p 80,443 <target>
```

Service Version Detection: Nmap can detect the version of services running on a target system or network. To do this, use the **-sV** option. For example:

```
phpCopy code
nmap -sV <target>
```

Operating System Detection: Nmap can detect the operating system used by a target system or network. To do this, use the **-O** option. For example:

```
mathematicaCopy code
nmap -O <target>
```

Output Formats: Nmap can generate output in various formats such as plain text, XML, and HTML. To specify an output format, use the **-o** option followed by the desired format. For example, to save the output in XML format, use the following command:

```
luaCopy code
nmap -oX output.xml <target>
```

Script Scanning: Nmap includes a scripting engine that can be used to automate tasks such as vulnerability scanning and banner grabbing. To use scripts, use the **—script** option followed by the name of the script. For example, to use the HTTP title script, use the following command:

```
cssCopy code
nmap --script http-title <target>
```

These are just some basic instructions for using Nmap. The tool is highly configurable and can be customized to suit specific needs. It is important to use Nmap ethically and with appropriate authorization, as it can be used for both legitimate and illegitimate purposes.

ntpq

ntpq is a command-line utility that is used to query NTP (Network Time Protocol) servers and retrieve information such as the IP address, hostname, and version of the NTP server. It is included with most NTP client packages and can also be downloaded separately from the official NTP support website: **https://support.ntp.org/bin/view/Support/DocumentationNtpq**.

Here are some instructions for using ntpq:

1. Launching ntpq: Open a terminal or command prompt and enter the command **ntpq** to launch the utility.
2. Querying NTP servers: Use the **-p** option to query NTP servers and display a list of their peers and synchronization status. For example:

```
cssCopy code
ntpq -p
```

This command will display the IP addresses, hostnames, and synchronization status of the NTP servers configured on your system.

Displaying NTP server version: Use the **-c** option followed by the **version** command to display the version of the NTP server. For example:

```
phpCopy code
ntpq -c version <target>
```

Replace **<target>** with the IP address or hostname of the NTP server you want to query.

Displaying NTP server status: Use the **-c** option followed by the **sysinfo** command to display information about the NTP server's status. For example:

```phpCopy code
ntpq -c sysinfo <target>
```

Replace **<target>** with the IP address or hostname of the NTP server you want to query.

Setting the NTP server: Use the **-c** option followed by the **host** command to set the NTP server. For example:

```phpCopy code
ntpq -c host <target>
```

Replace **<target>** with the IP address or hostname of the NTP server you want to set.

Exiting ntpq: To exit ntpq, type **quit** or **exit** at the prompt and press Enter.

These are just some basic instructions for using ntpq. The tool is highly configurable and can be customized to suit specific needs. It is important to use ntpq ethically and with appropriate authorization, as it can be used for both legitimate and illegitimate purposes.

showmount

showmount is a command-line utility used to query NFS (Network File System) servers and retrieve information about the file systems shared by the server. It is typically included with NFS client packages and can be run on a Linux, Unix, or macOS operating system.

Here are some instructions for using showmount:

1. Launching showmount: Open a terminal or command prompt and enter the command **showmount** to launch the utility.
2. Displaying shared file systems: Use the **-e** option to display a list of file systems shared by the NFS server. For example:

```php
phpCopy code
showmount -e <target>
```

Replace **<target>** with the IP address or hostname of the NFS server you want to query.

1. Displaying clients with access to shared file systems: Use the **-a** option to display a list of clients that have access to the shared file systems. For example:

```css
cssCopy code
showmount -a <target>
```

Replace **<target>** with the IP address or hostname of the NFS server you want to query.

1. Checking mount status of NFS file systems: Use the **-m** option to check the mount status of NFS file systems on a client machine. For example:

```php
phpCopy code
showmount -m <target>
```

Replace **<target>** with the IP address or hostname of the client machine you want to query.

1. Displaying help: Use the **—help** option to display help information about showmount and its options.
2. Exiting showmount: To exit showmount, type **ctrl+c** or **q** at the prompt and press Enter.

These are just some basic instructions for using showmount. The tool is highly configurable and can be customized to suit specific needs. It is important to use showmount ethically and with appropriate authorization, as it can be used for both legitimate and illegitimate purposes.

nfsstat

nfsstat is a command-line utility used to display statistical information about the use of NFS (Network File System) servers and clients. It provides information about the NFS version, server performance, and the number of operations performed on the server. The utility is typically included with most NFS client packages and can be run on a Linux, Unix, or macOS operating system.

Here are some instructions for using nfsstat:

1. Launching nfsstat: Open a terminal or command prompt and enter the command **nfsstat** to launch the utility.
2. Displaying server performance statistics: Use the **-s** option to display server performance statistics. For example:

```
Copy code
nfsstat -s
```

This command will display statistics such as the number of operations performed, the number of calls to the server, and the number of errors encountered.

1. Displaying client statistics: Use the **-c** option to display client statistics. For example:

```
rCopy code
nfsstat -c
```

This command will display statistics such as the number of RPC (Remote Procedure Call) calls sent to the server, the number of operations performed, and the number of errors encountered.

1. Displaying NFS version: Use the **-m** option to display the NFS version in use. For example:

```
Copy code
nfsstat -m
```

This command will display the NFS version in use, such as NFSv3 or NFSv4.

1. Displaying help: Use the **—help** option to display help information about nfsstat and its options.
2. Exiting nfsstat: To exit nfsstat, type **ctrl+c** or **q** at the prompt and press Enter.

These are just some basic instructions for using nfsstat. The tool is highly configurable and can be customized to suit specific needs. It is important to use nfsstat ethically and with appropriate authorization, as it can be used for both legitimate and illegitimate purposes.

Vulnerabilities identified through NTP and NFS Enumeration

NTP and NFS Enumeration can reveal a number of vulnerabilities that attackers can exploit to compromise a system or network. Here are some of the vulnerabilities that can be identified through NTP and NFS Enumeration:

1. Unauthorized access: NTP and NFS Enumeration can reveal NFS file systems that are improperly configured and can be accessed by unauthorized users. This can lead to unauthorized access and the exposure of sensitive data.

2. Weak authentication: NTP and NFS Enumeration can reveal systems that use weak or outdated authentication mechanisms, such as plain text passwords or no authentication at all. This can allow attackers to gain access to sensitive data and resources.

3. Denial-of-service attacks: NTP Enumeration can reveal systems that are vulnerable to NTP-based denial-of-service (DoS) attacks. Attackers can use NTP reflection attacks to flood a target system with NTP traffic, overwhelming it and making it unavailable.

4. Data tampering: NFS Enumeration can reveal systems that are vulnerable to data tampering attacks. Attackers can modify or delete files on an NFS file system, causing data loss or corruption.

5. Information disclosure: NTP and NFS Enumeration can reveal information about the target system, such as server and client IP addresses, network topology, and system configurations. This information can be used by attackers to plan more targeted attacks against the system or network.

These vulnerabilities can be mitigated through various countermeasures, such as properly configuring NFS file systems, implementing strong authentication mechanisms, and using firewalls to block NTP traffic from unauthorized sources. It is important to regularly perform NTP and NFS Enumeration to identify vulnerabilities and address them before they can be exploited by attackers.

Counter Measures

To prevent vulnerabilities identified through NTP and NFS Enumeration, organizations can implement various countermeasures. Here are some recommended countermeasures:

1. Configure NFS securely: Ensure that NFS file systems are properly configured with appropriate permissions and access controls to prevent unauthorized access. Use secure protocols like NFSv4 or Kerberos-based authentication to provide strong security for the NFS system.
2. Implement strong authentication mechanisms: Use strong authentication mechanisms like Secure Shell (SSH) or Transport Layer Security (TLS) to prevent unauthorized access to NTP or NFS servers. Implement multi-factor authentication to add an extra layer of security.
3. Implement firewall rules: Implement firewall rules to block NTP traffic from unauthorized sources. Only allow NTP traffic from trusted sources and limit the number of NTP queries allowed from each source.
4. Patch vulnerabilities: Ensure that all systems and software are patched and up-to-date to address known vulnerabilities in NTP and NFS software.
5. Monitor and analyze network traffic: Regularly monitor and analyze network traffic to identify any unusual or suspicious activity. Implement intrusion detection and prevention systems (IDPS) to detect and prevent malicious activity.
6. Use encryption: Use encryption to secure NTP and NFS communications. Implement Transport Layer Security (TLS) or Secure Sockets Layer (SSL) to protect data transmitted over the network.
7. Regularly perform vulnerability assessments: Regularly perform NTP and NFS Enumeration to identify vulnerabilities in the network and systems, and address them before they can be exploited by attackers.

By implementing these countermeasures, organizations can greatly reduce the risk of vulnerabilities identified through NTP and NFS Enumeration. It is important to regularly review and update security policies and procedures to ensure that they remain effective against the evolving threat landscape.

Discussion

NTP and NFS Enumeration are processes that involve gathering information about NTP and NFS servers on a target system or network. NTP Enumeration involves collecting details about NTP servers, such as IP addresses, versions, and configurations. NFS Enumeration, on the other hand, involves collecting details about NFS servers, such as file systems, permissions, and access controls.

Various tools are used for NTP and NFS Enumeration, such as Nmap, ntpq, sntp, showmount, nfsstat, and others. These tools allow security professionals to gather information about the network and identify potential vulnerabilities that can be exploited by attackers.

Some of the vulnerabilities that can be identified through NTP and NFS Enumeration include unauthorized access, weak authentication, denial-of-service attacks, data tampering, and information disclosure. To prevent these vulnerabilities, organizations can implement countermeasures such as configuring NFS file systems securely, implementing strong authentication mechanisms, and patching vulnerabilities.

Firewall rules can also be implemented to block NTP traffic from unauthorized sources, and the number of NTP queries allowed from each source can be limited to prevent denial-of-service attacks. Encryption protocols such as TLS and SSL can be used to secure NTP and NFS communications, protecting data transmitted over the network.

Regular vulnerability assessments for NTP and NFS Enumeration are important to identify vulnerabilities and address them before they can be exploited by attackers. Organizations should also monitor network traffic regularly to detect any unusual or suspicious activity.

In summary, NTP and NFS Enumeration are important processes for identifying potential vulnerabilities in a network. By using appropriate tools and implementing countermeasures, organizations can greatly reduce the risk of vulnerabilities and secure their systems and networks from potential attacks.

Quiz

1. What is NTP Enumeration?
2. What is NFS Enumeration?
3. What are some tools used for NTP Enumeration?
4. What are some tools used for NFS Enumeration?
5. What are some vulnerabilities that can be identified through NTP and NFS Enumeration?
6. How can organizations prevent unauthorized access to NFS file systems?
7. How can organizations prevent NTP-based denial-of-service attacks?
8. What is the role of encryption in securing NTP and NFS communications?
9. How often should organizations perform vulnerability assessments for NTP and NFS Enumeration?
10. What are some recommended countermeasures for NTP and NFS Enumeration vulnerabilities?

6

SMTP and DNS Enumeration

SMTP and DNS Enumeration are important techniques used in cybersecurity to gather information about a target system or network. SMTP Enumeration is the process of gathering information about Simple Mail Transfer Protocol (SMTP) servers, while DNS Enumeration is the process of gathering information about Domain Name System (DNS) servers.

SMTP Enumeration involves collecting details about SMTP servers, such as the email addresses of users, valid usernames, email relays, and configurations. This information can be used by attackers to identify potential vulnerabilities and launch targeted attacks.

DNS Enumeration, on the other hand, involves gathering information about DNS servers, such as hostnames, IP addresses, and domain names. This information can be used to map the network and identify potential vulnerabilities that can be exploited by attackers.

Various tools are used for SMTP and DNS Enumeration, such as Nmap, nslookup, dig, and others. These tools allow security professionals to gather information about the network and identify potential vulnerabilities that can be exploited by attackers.

Some of the vulnerabilities that can be identified through SMTP and DNS Enumeration include weak passwords, open relays, insecure configurations, and unsecured DNS zones. To prevent these vulnerabilities, organizations can implement countermeasures such as using strong passwords, securing SMTP servers, and configuring DNS servers securely.

In summary, SMTP and DNS Enumeration are important techniques used in cybersecurity to identify potential vulnerabilities in a target system or network. By using appropriate tools and implementing countermeasures, organizations can greatly reduce the risk of vulnerabilities and secure their systems and networks from potential attacks.

Tools used for SMTP and DNS Enumeration

Tools used for SMTP and DNS Enumeration include:

1. Nmap: Nmap is a popular port scanner tool that can be used for network exploration, vulnerability detection, and enumeration. It can be used for SMTP and DNS Enumeration by identifying open ports and collecting information about the target system or network. Nmap can be downloaded from **https://nmap.org/download.html**.

2. nslookup: nslookup is a command-line tool used for querying DNS servers to gather information about hostnames, IP addresses, and other DNS records. It can be used for DNS Enumeration by querying DNS servers to collect information about a target system or network. nslookup is typically included in most operating systems and does not require a separate download.

3. dig: dig is another command-line tool used for querying DNS servers to gather information about hostnames, IP addresses, and other DNS records. It can be used for DNS Enumeration by querying DNS servers to collect information about a target system or network. dig can be downloaded from **https://www.isc.org/download/**.

4. smtp-user-enum: smtp-user-enum is a tool that can be used for SMTP Enumeration by identifying valid usernames or user accounts on an SMTP server. It can be downloaded from **https://github.com/pentestmonkey/smtp-user-enum**.

5. smtpscan: smtpscan is another tool used for SMTP Enumeration by identifying open SMTP servers and collecting information about them.

It can be downloaded from **https://tools.kali.org/information-gatheri ng/smtpscan**.

By using appropriate tools such as Nmap, nslookup, dig, smtp-user-enum, and smtpscan, security professionals can gather information about the target system or network and identify potential vulnerabilities that can be exploited by attackers. It is important to note that these tools should only be used in a legal and ethical manner for security purposes.

Nmap

Nmap (Network Mapper) is a popular tool used for network exploration, vulnerability detection, and enumeration. It can be used for SMTP and DNS Enumeration by identifying open ports and collecting information about the target system or network. Here are some instructions on how to use Nmap:

1. Install Nmap: Nmap can be downloaded from the official website **https://nmap.org/download.html**. The website provides installation packages for various operating systems.
2. Identify the target: Determine the target IP address or hostname that you want to scan.
3. Run the scan: Open a command prompt or terminal and enter the following command:

```
nmap [target IP address or hostname]
```

1. This will run a basic scan on the target system and identify open ports and services.
2. Specify scan options: Nmap offers various scan options that can be used to gather more detailed information about the target system. Some commonly used scan options include:

- **-sS**: TCP SYN scan to identify open ports
- **-sU**: UDP scan to identify open UDP ports
- **-sV**: Version detection to identify the versions of services running on open ports
- **-A**: Aggressive scan to identify operating system, services, and versions

To use these scan options, enter the following command:

```
nmap [scan option] [target IP address or hostname]
```

Output results: Nmap offers various output options to view the scan results. By default, the scan results are displayed in the command prompt or terminal window. To save the results to a file, enter the following command:

```
nmap [scan option] [target IP address or hostname] -oN [output
file name]
```

This will save the scan results in a specified file in normal format.

In conclusion, Nmap is a powerful tool used for network exploration and enumeration. By using appropriate scan options, security professionals can gather information about the target system or network and identify potential vulnerabilities that can be exploited by attackers. It is important to note that Nmap should only be used in a legal and ethical manner for security purposes.

nslookup

nslookup is a command-line tool used for querying DNS servers to gather information about hostnames, IP addresses, and other DNS records. It can be used for DNS Enumeration by querying DNS servers to collect information about a target system or network. Here are some instructions on how to use nslookup:

1. Open Command Prompt or Terminal: nslookup is a command-line tool and can be run from the Command Prompt on Windows or Terminal on macOS and Linux.
2. Determine the target: Identify the target hostname or IP address that you want to query.
3. Run nslookup: Enter the following command and replace "example.com" with the target hostname or IP address:

```
nslookup example.com
```

1. This will run nslookup and display the target IP address and other DNS records associated with the target.
2. Query a specific DNS server: By default, nslookup queries the DNS server that is configured on the local machine. To query a specific DNS server, enter the following command and replace "8.8.8.8" with the IP address of the DNS server you want to query:

```
nslookup example.com 8.8.8.8
```

1. This will query the specified DNS server and display the target IP address and other DNS records associated with the target.
2. Reverse DNS lookup: nslookup can also be used to perform a reverse DNS lookup, which returns the hostname associated with a given IP address. To perform a reverse DNS lookup, enter the following command and replace "192.168.1.1" with the target IP address:

```
nslookup 192.168.1.1
```

This will return the hostname associated with the target IP address.

In conclusion, nslookup is a simple but powerful tool used for DNS Enumeration. By querying DNS servers, security professionals can gather information about the target system or network and identify potential vulnerabilities that can be exploited by attackers. It is important to note that nslookup should only be used in a legal and ethical manner for security purposes.

dig

dig (domain information groper) is a command-line tool used for querying DNS servers to gather information about hostnames, IP addresses, and other DNS records. It can be used for DNS Enumeration by querying DNS servers to collect information about a target system or network. Here are some instructions on how to use dig:

1. Open Command Prompt or Terminal: dig is a command-line tool and can be run from the Command Prompt on Windows or Terminal on macOS and Linux.
2. Determine the target: Identify the target hostname or IP address that you want to query.
3. Run dig: Enter the following command and replace "example.com" with the target hostname or IP address:

```
dig example.com
```

1. This will run dig and display the target IP address and other DNS records associated with the target.
2. Query a specific DNS server: By default, dig queries the DNS server that is configured on the local machine. To query a specific DNS server, enter the following command and replace "8.8.8.8" with the IP address of the

DNS server you want to query:

```
dig example.com @8.8.8.8
```

1. This will query the specified DNS server and display the target IP address and other DNS records associated with the target.
2. Reverse DNS lookup: dig can also be used to perform a reverse DNS lookup, which returns the hostname associated with a given IP address. To perform a reverse DNS lookup, enter the following command and replace "192.168.1.1" with the target IP address:

```
dig -x 192.168.1.1
```

This will return the hostname associated with the target IP address.

In conclusion, dig is a versatile tool used for DNS Enumeration. By querying DNS servers, security professionals can gather information about the target system or network and identify potential vulnerabilities that can be exploited by attackers. It is important to note that dig should only be used in a legal and ethical manner for security purposes.

smtp-user-enum

smtp-user-enum is a tool used for SMTP Enumeration, which is the process of identifying valid email addresses on a target system or network. Here are some instructions on how to use smtp-user-enum:

1. Install smtp-user-enum: smtp-user-enum is included in many security-focused Linux distributions, such as Kali Linux. If it is not already installed on your system, you can download it from the official GitHub

page.

2. Determine the target: Identify the target SMTP server or IP address that you want to enumerate.

3. Run smtp-user-enum: Enter the following command and replace "smtp.example.com" with the target SMTP server or IP address:

```
smtp-user-enum -U /path/to/usernames.txt -t smtp.example.com
```

1. This will run smtp-user-enum and enumerate the valid usernames associated with the target SMTP server. The -U flag specifies the path to a file containing a list of usernames to test.

2. Optional flags: smtp-user-enum also supports additional flags that can be used to customize the enumeration process. For example, the -p flag can be used to specify a different port to use for SMTP (the default is 25), and the -M flag can be used to specify the maximum number of concurrent connections to use.

3. Analyze the results: Once smtp-user-enum has completed the enumeration process, it will display a list of valid usernames associated with the target SMTP server. This information can be used to identify potential targets for social engineering attacks, such as phishing.

In conclusion, smtp-user-enum is a powerful tool used for SMTP Enumeration. It can be used to identify valid email addresses on a target system or network, which can be used to launch social engineering attacks or brute-force attacks on login pages. It is important to note that smtp-user-enum should only be used in a legal and ethical manner for security purposes.

smtpscan

smtpscan is a tool used for SMTP Enumeration, which is the process of identifying valid email addresses on a target system or network. Here are some instructions on how to use smtpscan:

1. Install smtpscan: smtpscan is included in many security-focused Linux distributions, such as Kali Linux. If it is not already installed on your system, you can download it from the official GitHub page.
2. Determine the target: Identify the target SMTP server or IP address that you want to enumerate.
3. Run smtpscan: Enter the following command and replace "smtp.example.com" with the target SMTP server or IP address:

```
smtpscan -s smtp.example.com
```

1. This will run smtpscan and enumerate the valid usernames associated with the target SMTP server. The -s flag specifies the hostname or IP address of the SMTP server to scan.
2. Optional flags: smtpscan also supports additional flags that can be used to customize the enumeration process. For example, the -t flag can be used to specify the number of threads to use for scanning (the default is 4), and the -v flag can be used to enable verbose output.
3. Analyze the results: Once smtpscan has completed the enumeration process, it will display a list of valid usernames associated with the target SMTP server. This information can be used to identify potential targets for social engineering attacks, such as phishing.

In conclusion, smtpscan is a powerful tool used for SMTP Enumeration. It can be used to identify valid email addresses on a target system or network, which can be used to launch social engineering attacks or brute-force attacks on login pages. It is important to note that smtpscan should only be used in a legal and ethical manner for security purposes.

Vulnerabilities identified through SMTP and DNS Enumeration

SMTP and DNS Enumeration can help identify vulnerabilities in a system or network. Here are some vulnerabilities that can be identified through SMTP and DNS Enumeration:

1. User enumeration: SMTP and DNS Enumeration can be used to identify valid usernames and email addresses associated with a target system or network. Attackers can use this information to launch brute-force attacks on login pages or launch phishing attacks.
2. Misconfigured DNS records: DNS Enumeration can identify misconfigured DNS records that can be exploited by attackers. For example, a misconfigured MX record can allow an attacker to intercept emails intended for the target domain.
3. Open SMTP relay: SMTP Enumeration can identify open SMTP relays that can be exploited by attackers to send spam or launch phishing attacks.
4. Outdated software: SMTP and DNS Enumeration can identify outdated software versions on a target system or network. These outdated versions can be exploited by attackers using known vulnerabilities to gain unauthorized access.
5. Information leakage: SMTP and DNS Enumeration can reveal sensitive information about a target system or network. For example, SMTP Enumeration can reveal the software version used by the SMTP server, which can be used to identify known vulnerabilities.

In conclusion, SMTP and DNS Enumeration can help identify vulnerabilities that can be exploited by attackers. It is important to regularly perform Enumeration on your systems and networks to identify potential vulnerabilities and take steps to mitigate them.

Counter Measures

Here are some countermeasures that can be implemented to protect against SMTP and DNS Enumeration:

1. Restrict access: Restrict access to SMTP and DNS servers to authorized personnel only. Use strong passwords and multi-factor authentication to prevent unauthorized access.
2. Implement rate limiting: Implement rate limiting on DNS and SMTP servers to prevent brute-force attacks.
3. Disable open relays: Disable open SMTP relays to prevent attackers from using them to send spam or launch phishing attacks.
4. Monitor DNS records: Monitor DNS records for changes and ensure that they are properly configured to prevent misconfigurations that can be exploited by attackers.
5. Keep software up to date: Keep software on DNS and SMTP servers up to date with the latest security patches to prevent exploitation of known vulnerabilities.
6. Use network segmentation: Use network segmentation to isolate DNS and SMTP servers from other systems and networks to prevent attackers from gaining unauthorized access.
7. Hide software version: Hide the software version of DNS and SMTP servers to prevent attackers from identifying known vulnerabilities.
8. Implement DNSSEC: Implement DNSSEC (DNS Security Extensions) to add an additional layer of security to DNS records.

In conclusion, implementing these countermeasures can help protect against SMTP and DNS Enumeration. It is important to regularly review and update security measures to stay ahead of evolving threats.

Discussion

SMTP and DNS Enumeration are common techniques used by cyber attackers to gather information about a target system or network. SMTP Enumeration involves querying the SMTP server to identify email addresses associated with the target system or network, while DNS Enumeration involves querying the DNS to gather information about the system or network, such as IP addresses, domain names, and subdomains.

Tools such as smtp-user-enum, smtpscan, Nmap, nslookup, and dig are commonly used for SMTP and DNS Enumeration. However, it is important to note that these tools should only be used in an ethical hacking context.

SMTP and DNS Enumeration can identify vulnerabilities such as open relays, outdated software, and information leakage. These vulnerabilities can be exploited by attackers to gain unauthorized access to the system or network.

Countermeasures can be implemented to protect against SMTP and DNS Enumeration. For SMTP Enumeration, it is important to restrict access, implement rate limiting, and disable open relays. For DNS Enumeration, it is important to monitor DNS records, keep software up to date, and implement network segmentation.

Best practices for securing SMTP and DNS servers include using strong passwords, implementing multi-factor authentication, keeping software up to date with security patches, and hiding the software version of servers to prevent attackers from identifying known vulnerabilities.

Overall, understanding SMTP and DNS Enumeration techniques and implementing appropriate countermeasures and best practices can help protect against potential vulnerabilities and attacks. It is important to regularly review and update security measures to stay ahead of evolving threats.

Quiz

1. What is SMTP Enumeration?
2. What is DNS Enumeration?
3. What are some tools used for SMTP Enumeration?

4. What are some tools used for DNS Enumeration?
5. What vulnerabilities can be identified through SMTP Enumeration?
6. What vulnerabilities can be identified through DNS Enumeration?
7. What countermeasures can be implemented to protect against SMTP Enumeration?
8. What countermeasures can be implemented to protect against DNS Enumeration?
9. Why is SMTP and DNS Enumeration important in cybersecurity?
10. What are some best practices for securing SMTP and DNS servers?

7

Other Enumeration Techniques

Other Enumeration Techniques in cybersecurity include NetBIOS Enumeration, SNMP Enumeration, LDAP Enumeration, NTP and NFS Enumeration. NetBIOS Enumeration involves querying the NetBIOS protocol to gather information about a target system or network, while SNMP Enumeration involves querying the Simple Network Management Protocol (SNMP) to gather information about network devices. LDAP Enumeration involves querying the Lightweight Directory Access Protocol (LDAP) to gather information about user and group accounts within an LDAP directory.

NTP and NFS Enumeration involve querying the Network Time Protocol (NTP) and the Network File System (NFS) to gather information about the target system or network, such as available shares and time synchronization information.

Tools such as Nmap, NBTScan, JXplorer, and SolarWinds Network Performance Monitor are commonly used for these Enumeration techniques. These tools should only be used in an ethical hacking context.

Vulnerabilities that can be identified through these Enumeration techniques include misconfigured settings, outdated software, and information leakage. Countermeasures to protect against these vulnerabilities include monitoring network traffic, keeping software up to date, implementing network segmentation, and restricting access.

Overall, understanding these Enumeration techniques and implementing appropriate countermeasures can help protect against potential vulnerabilities and attacks. It is important to regularly review and update security measures to stay ahead of evolving threats.

IPsec Enumeration

IPsec Enumeration is the process of gathering information about the IPsec settings and configurations of a target system or network. IPsec (Internet Protocol Security) is a set of protocols used to secure Internet Protocol (IP) communications. The main objective of IPsec Enumeration is to identify vulnerabilities in IPsec configurations that can be exploited by attackers to gain unauthorized access to the system or network.

Tools such as IKE-Scan and IKEProbe are commonly used for IPsec Enumeration. IKE-Scan sends IKE (Internet Key Exchange) requests to the target system or network to gather information about the supported encryption algorithms, hash functions, and other parameters. IKEProbe, on the other hand, sends malformed IKE packets to the target system or network to test for known vulnerabilities.

Vulnerabilities that can be identified through IPsec Enumeration include weak encryption algorithms, outdated software, and misconfigured settings. Countermeasures to protect against these vulnerabilities include implementing strong encryption algorithms, keeping software up to date, and configuring IPsec settings correctly.

Overall, understanding IPsec Enumeration techniques and implementing appropriate countermeasures can help protect against potential vulnerabilities and attacks. It is important to regularly review and update security measures to stay ahead of evolving threats.

VoIP Enumeration

VoIP Enumeration is the process of gathering information about the Voice over Internet Protocol (VoIP) settings and configurations of a target system or network. VoIP is a technology that allows voice communication over the

Internet, and it is commonly used in business and personal communications. The main objective of VoIP Enumeration is to identify vulnerabilities in VoIP configurations that can be exploited by attackers to gain unauthorized access to the system or network.

Tools such as Viproy and SIPVicious are commonly used for VoIP Enumeration. Viproy is an open-source VoIP Penetration Testing and Exploitation Kit that can be used to identify vulnerabilities in VoIP systems. SIPVicious, on the other hand, is a set of tools for auditing and attacking SIP (Session Initiation Protocol) based VoIP systems.

Vulnerabilities that can be identified through VoIP Enumeration include weak passwords, misconfigured settings, and outdated software. Countermeasures to protect against these vulnerabilities include implementing strong passwords, keeping software up to date, and configuring VoIP settings correctly.

Overall, understanding VoIP Enumeration techniques and implementing appropriate countermeasures can help protect against potential vulnerabilities and attacks. It is important to regularly review and update security measures to stay ahead of evolving threats.

RPC Enumeration

RPC Enumeration is the process of gathering information about the Remote Procedure Call (RPC) settings and configurations of a target system or network. RPC is a protocol that enables communication between different processes on a system or network. The main objective of RPC Enumeration is to identify vulnerabilities in RPC configurations that can be exploited by attackers to gain unauthorized access to the system or network.

Tools such as Rpcclient and Enum4linux are commonly used for RPC Enumeration. Rpcclient is a tool that allows users to execute commands on an RPC server and retrieve information about the server's configuration. Enum4linux, on the other hand, is a tool that automates the process of enumerating RPC shares on a target system or network.

Vulnerabilities that can be identified through RPC Enumeration include weak authentication mechanisms, open shares, and outdated software. Countermeasures to protect against these vulnerabilities include implementing strong authentication mechanisms, restricting access to sensitive shares, and keeping software up to date.

Overall, understanding RPC Enumeration techniques and implementing appropriate countermeasures can help protect against potential vulnerabilities and attacks. It is important to regularly review and update security measures to stay ahead of evolving threats.

Unix/Linux Enumeration

Unix/Linux Enumeration is the process of gathering information about a Unix or Linux system's settings and configurations. The main objective of Unix/Linux Enumeration is to identify potential vulnerabilities and attack vectors that can be exploited by attackers to gain unauthorized access to the system or network.

Tools such as Nmap, LinEnum, and Unix-privesc-check are commonly used for Unix/Linux Enumeration. Nmap is a network scanning tool that can be used to identify open ports and running services on a Unix/Linux system. LinEnum is a script that automates the process of enumerating a Unix/Linux system's settings and configurations, including identifying user accounts, open ports, and system information. Unix-privesc-check is a tool that scans a Unix/Linux system and identifies potential privilege escalation vulnerabilities.

Vulnerabilities that can be identified through Unix/Linux Enumeration include weak user authentication, outdated software, and misconfigured settings. Countermeasures to protect against these vulnerabilities include implementing strong user authentication, keeping software up to date, and configuring settings correctly.

Overall, understanding Unix/Linux Enumeration techniques and implementing appropriate countermeasures can help protect against potential vulnerabilities and attacks. It is important to regularly review and update security measures to stay ahead of evolving threats.

Telnet Enumeration

Telnet Enumeration is the process of gathering information about the Telnet settings and configurations of a target system or network. Telnet is a protocol that enables remote access to a system or network. The main objective of Telnet Enumeration is to identify potential vulnerabilities in the Telnet configurations that can be exploited by attackers to gain unauthorized access to the system or network.

Tools such as Nmap and Telnet are commonly used for Telnet Enumeration. Nmap is a network scanning tool that can be used to identify open ports on a system, including Telnet ports. Telnet is a command-line tool that can be used to connect to a Telnet port and execute commands on the system.

Vulnerabilities that can be identified through Telnet Enumeration include weak authentication mechanisms, plaintext transmission of sensitive data, and open Telnet ports. Countermeasures to protect against these vulnerabilities include implementing strong authentication mechanisms, using secure alternatives to Telnet such as SSH, and restricting access to Telnet ports.

Overall, understanding Telnet Enumeration techniques and implementing appropriate countermeasures can help protect against potential vulnerabilities and attacks. It is important to regularly review and update security measures to stay ahead of evolving threats.

FTP Enumeration

FTP (File Transfer Protocol) Enumeration is the process of gathering information about the FTP settings and configurations of a target system or network. FTP is a standard network protocol used to transfer files between a client and a server. The main objective of FTP Enumeration is to identify potential vulnerabilities in the FTP configurations that can be exploited by attackers to gain unauthorized access to the system or network.

Tools such as Nmap, Netcat, and FTP are commonly used for FTP Enumeration. Nmap is a network scanning tool that can be used to identify open ports on a system, including FTP ports. Netcat is a command-line tool that can be used to connect to an FTP port and execute commands on the system. FTP is a protocol that can be used to connect to an FTP server and transfer files between the client and server.

Vulnerabilities that can be identified through FTP Enumeration include weak authentication mechanisms, unencrypted transmission of sensitive data, and open FTP ports. Countermeasures to protect against these vulnerabilities include implementing strong authentication mechanisms, using secure alternatives to FTP such as SFTP or FTPS, and restricting access to FTP ports.

Overall, understanding FTP Enumeration techniques and implementing appropriate countermeasures can help protect against potential vulnerabilities and attacks. It is important to regularly review and update security measures to stay ahead of evolving threats.

TFTP Enumeration

TFTP (Trivial File Transfer Protocol) Enumeration is the process of gathering information about the TFTP settings and configurations of a target system or network. TFTP is a simple file transfer protocol commonly used in network booting and firmware updates. The main objective of TFTP Enumeration is to identify potential vulnerabilities in the TFTP configurations that can be exploited by attackers to gain unauthorized access to the system or network.

Tools such as Nmap and TFTP are commonly used for TFTP Enumeration. Nmap is a network scanning tool that can be used to identify open ports on a system, including TFTP ports. TFTP is a protocol that can be used to connect to a TFTP server and transfer files between the client and server.

Vulnerabilities that can be identified through TFTP Enumeration include weak authentication mechanisms, unencrypted transmission of sensitive data, and open TFTP ports. Countermeasures to protect against these vulnerabilities include implementing strong authentication mechanisms, using secure alternatives to TFTP such as SCP or SFTP, and restricting access to TFTP ports.

Overall, understanding TFTP Enumeration techniques and implementing appropriate countermeasures can help protect against potential vulnerabilities and attacks. It is important to regularly review and update security measures to stay ahead of evolving threats.

SMB Enumeration

SMB (Server Message Block) Enumeration is the process of gathering information about the SMB settings and configurations of a target system or network. SMB is a network protocol used for file sharing, printing, and communication between computers. The main objective of SMB Enumeration is to identify potential vulnerabilities in the SMB configurations that can be exploited by attackers to gain unauthorized access to the system or network.

Tools such as Nmap, NetBIOS, and SMB are commonly used for SMB Enumeration. Nmap is a network scanning tool that can be used to identify open ports on a system, including SMB ports. NetBIOS is a protocol used to identify devices on a network, and SMB can be used to connect to an SMB server and browse shared folders and resources.

Vulnerabilities that can be identified through SMB Enumeration include weak authentication mechanisms, open SMB ports, and unsecured file shares. Countermeasures to protect against these vulnerabilities include implementing strong authentication mechanisms, securing file shares with appropriate permissions, and using secure alternatives to SMB such as SFTP or SCP.

Overall, understanding SMB Enumeration techniques and implementing appropriate countermeasures can help protect against potential vulnerabilities and attacks. It is important to regularly review and update security measures to stay ahead of evolving threats.

IPv6 Enumeration

IPv6 Enumeration is the process of collecting information about a target system or network's IPv6 address scheme, including network topology, address allocation, and device configurations. With the increasing adoption of IPv6, it has become important to understand how to conduct IPv6 Enumeration and identify potential vulnerabilities that can be exploited by attackers.

Tools such as Nmap and THC-IPv6 are commonly used for IPv6 Enumeration. Nmap is a network scanning tool that can be used to scan for open ports on IPv6 addresses, while THC-IPv6 is a suite of tools specifically designed for IPv6 network reconnaissance and security testing.

Vulnerabilities that can be identified through IPv6 Enumeration include weak authentication mechanisms, unsecured configurations, and open ports. Countermeasures to protect against these vulnerabilities include implementing strong authentication mechanisms, securing configurations with appropriate permissions, and using firewalls to restrict access to open ports.

Overall, understanding IPv6 Enumeration techniques and implementing appropriate countermeasures can help protect against potential vulnerabilities and attacks. It is important to regularly review and update security measures to stay ahead of evolving threats in the rapidly changing world of cybersecurity.

BGP Enumeration

BGP (Border Gateway Protocol) Enumeration is the process of collecting information about BGP-enabled devices and their configurations within a target network. BGP is a routing protocol used for exchanging routing information between different networks and is commonly used by Internet Service Providers (ISPs) and large organizations to manage their network traffic.

Tools such as Nmap, BGPlay, and BGPView are commonly used for BGP Enumeration. Nmap can be used to scan for open BGP ports, while BGPlay and BGPView can be used to visualize BGP routing information and identify potential misconfigurations or vulnerabilities in the network.

Vulnerabilities that can be identified through BGP Enumeration include misconfigured routing policies, insecure configurations, and unsecured BGP sessions. Countermeasures to protect against these vulnerabilities include implementing secure BGP configurations, using cryptographic mechanisms to protect BGP sessions, and regularly reviewing routing policies and configurations.

Overall, understanding BGP Enumeration techniques and implementing appropriate countermeasures can help protect against potential vulnerabilities and attacks. It is important to regularly review and update security measures to stay ahead of evolving threats in the rapidly changing world of cybersecurity.

Discussion

Enumeration is a critical aspect of cybersecurity that involves collecting information about a target system or network. The information collected during enumeration can help identify potential vulnerabilities and attack vectors that can be exploited by attackers. The different types of enumeration techniques include user enumeration, network enumeration, operating system enumeration, service enumeration, file and share enumeration, LDAP enumeration, DNS enumeration, NetBIOS enumeration, SNMP enumeration, NTP and NFS enumeration, SMTP and DNS enumeration, IPsec enumeration, VoIP enumeration, RPC enumeration, Unix/Linux enumeration, Telnet enumeration, FTP enumeration, TFTP enumeration, SMB enumeration, IPv6 enumeration, and BGP enumeration.

To prevent enumeration attacks, it is essential to follow best practices such as using strong passwords, limiting user access, and disabling unused services. Other measures to detect and mitigate enumeration attacks include monitoring network traffic, configuring firewalls and intrusion detection systems, and using encryption and other security measures to protect sensitive data.

Countermeasures for specific enumeration techniques vary depending on the technique used. For example, to prevent NetBIOS enumeration, one should disable the NetBIOS over TCP/IP protocol, use VPNs to encrypt network traffic, and restrict access to network shares. Similarly, to prevent SNMP enumeration, one should use SNMPv3, use strong passwords and authentication mechanisms, and monitor network traffic for unusual activity.

Overall, understanding the different types of enumeration techniques and implementing appropriate countermeasures can help improve network security and prevent successful attacks. It is essential to remain vigilant and stay up-to-date with the latest cybersecurity trends to ensure that systems and networks are adequately protected.

Quiz

1. What is IPsec Enumeration?
2. What is VoIP Enumeration?
3. What is RPC Enumeration?
4. What is Unix/Linux Enumeration?
5. What is Telnet Enumeration?
6. What is FTP Enumeration?
7. What is TFTP Enumeration?
8. What is SMB Enumeration?
9. What is IPv6 Enumeration?
10. What is BGP Enumeration?

8

Enumeration Countermeasures

Enumeration is a process of collecting information about a target system or network that can be used to identify potential vulnerabilities and attack vectors. While it can be used for legitimate purposes, enumeration can also be used by attackers to gain unauthorized access or to launch attacks.

To protect against enumeration, it is important to implement appropriate countermeasures. Some general countermeasures that can be applied to multiple types of enumeration include implementing strong authentication mechanisms, regularly reviewing and updating security configurations, and using firewalls to restrict access to open ports.

For specific types of enumeration, there are additional countermeasures that can be implemented. For example, to protect against SNMP Enumeration, it is recommended to restrict SNMP access to trusted hosts, use SNMPv3 with encryption and authentication, and regularly review SNMP configurations. Similarly, to protect against LDAP Enumeration, it is recommended to implement secure LDAP configurations, use strong passwords, and restrict access to LDAP directories.

Overall, the key to protecting against enumeration is to understand the types of enumeration techniques that may be used against a system or network, and to implement appropriate countermeasures to mitigate potential vulnerabilities. Regular review and updating of security measures are also important to stay ahead of evolving threats in the rapidly changing world of cybersecurity.

Best practices to prevent Enumeration

Preventing enumeration is a critical aspect of network security. Here are some best practices to prevent enumeration:

1. Implement strong access controls: Ensure that only authorized personnel have access to sensitive data and network resources. Use access controls such as firewalls, intrusion prevention systems, and VPNs to protect against unauthorized access.

2. Implement encryption: Use encryption technologies to protect data in transit and at rest. This includes encrypting communications between devices, encrypting sensitive data on storage devices, and using encrypted authentication methods.

3. Use strong passwords: Implement strong password policies to prevent brute-force attacks. Encourage users to create complex passwords that are difficult to guess or crack.

4. Regularly review and update configurations: Ensure that configurations for all devices and applications are up-to-date and meet industry standards. Regularly review and update configurations to address vulnerabilities and emerging threats.

5. Limit access to network resources: Restrict access to network resources and services to only those who need them. This includes disabling unnecessary services and limiting access to shared files and folders.

6. Conduct regular security assessments: Perform regular security assessments, including vulnerability scans and penetration testing, to identify and address weaknesses in the network.

7. Educate users: Educate users about the risks of enumeration and how to identify and report suspicious activity. Train them on best practices for creating strong passwords, identifying phishing scams, and using security protocols.

By implementing these best practices, organizations can significantly reduce the risk of enumeration and protect their networks from unauthorized access and data breaches.

Techniques to detect and mitigate Enumeration attacks

Here are some techniques to detect and mitigate enumeration attacks:

1. Monitor network traffic: Use network monitoring tools to detect suspicious activity on the network, such as excessive requests for information or repeated failed login attempts.
2. Implement intrusion detection and prevention systems: IDS and IPS systems can detect and block malicious traffic, such as port scans and brute-force attacks.
3. Implement logging and alerting: Configure logging and alerting systems to notify administrators of suspicious activity, such as failed login attempts or multiple requests for the same resource.
4. Use honeypots: Deploy honeypots on the network to attract attackers and identify their tactics and techniques.
5. Implement rate limiting: Implement rate limiting on network services to prevent brute-force attacks and other types of enumeration.
6. Use firewalls: Configure firewalls to block unnecessary network traffic and restrict access to sensitive data and resources.
7. Implement access controls: Use access controls, such as RBAC (Role-Based Access Control) and ABAC (Attribute-Based Access Control), to restrict access to sensitive data and resources.
8. Keep software up-to-date: Keep software and systems up-to-date with the latest security patches and updates to prevent known vulnerabilities from being exploited.
9. Educate users: Educate users about the risks of enumeration and how to identify and report suspicious activity. Train them on best practices for creating strong passwords, identifying phishing scams, and using security protocols.

By implementing these techniques, organizations can detect and mitigate enumeration attacks and prevent unauthorized access to their networks and resources.

Countermeasures for specific Enumeration techniques

Here are some countermeasures for specific enumeration techniques:

1. User Enumeration: Use strong passwords and implement account lockout policies to prevent brute-force attacks. Limit the amount of information available to users, such as hiding email addresses from public directories.
2. Network Enumeration: Implement firewalls to block unnecessary traffic and limit access to sensitive data and resources. Disable unnecessary services and ports to reduce the attack surface.
3. OS Enumeration: Implement intrusion detection and prevention systems to detect and block malicious traffic, such as port scans and fingerprinting techniques. Keep systems up-to-date with the latest security patches and updates.
4. Service Enumeration: Disable unnecessary services and ports to reduce the attack surface. Implement intrusion detection and prevention systems to detect and block malicious traffic.
5. File and Share Enumeration: Implement access controls to restrict access to sensitive data and resources. Limit the amount of information available to users, such as hiding file and folder names from public directories.
6. LDAP Enumeration: Use strong passwords and implement account lockout policies to prevent brute-force attacks. Implement access controls to restrict access to sensitive data and resources.
7. DNS Enumeration: Use firewalls to block unnecessary traffic and limit access to sensitive data and resources. Implement intrusion detection and prevention systems to detect and block malicious traffic.
8. SNMP Enumeration: Implement strong authentication and access controls to restrict access to SNMP services. Use firewalls to block unneces-

sary traffic and limit access to sensitive data and resources.

9. NTP and NFS Enumeration: Implement firewalls to block unnecessary traffic and limit access to sensitive data and resources. Use encryption to protect data transmitted over the network.

By implementing these countermeasures, organizations can mitigate the risks associated with specific enumeration techniques and protect their networks and resources from unauthorized access and data breaches.

Discussion

In order to prevent Enumeration attacks, there are some general counter-measures that can be taken. Implementing strong authentication measures is one such measure. This includes requiring complex passwords, enforcing password changes on a regular basis, and implementing multi-factor authen-tication. Additionally, access to sensitive information should be limited to authorized personnel only. Regularly updating and patching systems can also help prevent Enumeration attacks, as can implementing firewalls and intrusion detection systems.

User enumeration can be prevented by implementing strong password policies. This includes requiring complex passwords, enforcing password changes on a regular basis, and implementing account lockout policies. Limiting the amount of information provided in error messages can also help prevent user enumeration.

Network enumeration can be prevented by implementing secure network configurations, using firewalls, and regularly scanning and monitoring network activity. This includes disabling unnecessary services, regularly mon-itoring and updating network configurations, and implementing intrusion detection systems.

OS enumeration can be mitigated by implementing secure OS configurations, regularly updating and patching systems, and implementing firewalls and intrusion detection systems. This includes disabling unnecessary services and implementing access controls to prevent unauthorized access to sensitive information.

Countermeasures to prevent service enumeration include disabling unnecessary services, using secure service configurations, and regularly monitoring and updating services. Additionally, implementing intrusion detection systems and firewalls can help prevent unauthorized access to sensitive information.

File and share enumeration can be prevented by using secure file and share configurations, regularly monitoring and updating file and share permissions, and implementing firewalls and intrusion detection systems. This includes disabling unnecessary file and share services and implementing access controls to prevent unauthorized access to sensitive information.

LDAP enumeration can be prevented by implementing secure LDAP configurations, using firewalls, and regularly monitoring and updating LDAP permissions. This includes disabling unnecessary LDAP services and implementing access controls to prevent unauthorized access to sensitive information.

DNS enumeration can be mitigated by implementing secure DNS configurations, regularly monitoring and updating DNS records, and using firewalls. This includes implementing access controls to prevent unauthorized access to sensitive information and disabling unnecessary DNS services.

Countermeasures to prevent NTP and NFS enumeration include implementing secure configurations, using firewalls and intrusion detection systems, and regularly monitoring and updating systems. This includes disabling unnecessary NTP and NFS services and implementing access controls to prevent unauthorized access to sensitive information.

SMTP and DNS enumeration can be prevented by implementing secure configurations, using firewalls and intrusion detection systems, and regularly monitoring and updating systems. Additionally, using strong authentication measures can prevent unauthorized access to sensitive information. This includes implementing access controls to prevent unauthorized access to sensitive information and disabling unnecessary SMTP and DNS services.

Quiz

1. What are some general countermeasures to prevent Enumeration attacks? Answer: General countermeasures to prevent Enumeration attacks include implementing strong authentication measures, limiting access to sensitive information, regularly updating and patching systems, and implementing firewalls and intrusion detection systems.
2. How can user enumeration be prevented? Answer: User enumeration can be prevented by implementing strong password policies, using account lockout policies, and limiting the amount of information provided in error messages.
3. What can be done to prevent network enumeration? Answer: Network enumeration can be prevented by implementing secure network configurations, using firewalls, and regularly scanning and monitoring network activity.
4. How can OS enumeration be mitigated? Answer: OS enumeration can be mitigated by implementing secure OS configurations, regularly updating and patching systems, and implementing firewalls and intrusion detection systems.
5. What countermeasures can be used to prevent service enumeration? Answer: Countermeasures to prevent service enumeration include disabling unnecessary services, using secure service configurations, and regularly monitoring and updating services.
6. How can file and share enumeration be prevented? Answer: File and share enumeration can be prevented by using secure file and share configurations, regularly monitoring and updating file and share permissions, and implementing firewalls and intrusion detection systems.
7. What can be done to prevent LDAP enumeration? Answer: LDAP enumeration can be prevented by implementing secure LDAP configurations, using firewalls, and regularly monitoring and updating LDAP permissions.
8. How can DNS enumeration be mitigated? Answer: DNS enumeration can be mitigated by implementing secure DNS configurations, regularly

monitoring and updating DNS records, and using firewalls.

9. What are some countermeasures to prevent NTP and NFS enumeration? Answer: Countermeasures to prevent NTP and NFS enumeration include implementing secure configurations, using firewalls and intrusion detection systems, and regularly monitoring and updating systems.

10. How can SMTP and DNS enumeration be prevented? Answer: SMTP and DNS enumeration can be prevented by implementing secure configurations, using firewalls and intrusion detection systems, and regularly monitoring and updating systems. Additionally, using strong authentication measures can prevent unauthorized access to sensitive information.

If you've read my book

If you've read my book, I would be grateful if you could take a moment to leave an honest review on Amazon. Your review will not only help other readers make an informed decision but also provide valuable feedback to me as an author. Thank you for taking

Introduction Quiz Solutions

1. What is enumeration in cybersecurity? Answer: Enumeration is the process of collecting information about a target system or network, such as usernames, IP addresses, open ports, and services, in order to identify potential vulnerabilities that can be exploited.

2. What are the types of enumeration? Answer: The types of enumeration techniques used in cybersecurity include User Enumeration, Network Enumeration, Operating System (OS) Enumeration, Service Enumeration, File and Share Enumeration, and LDAP Enumeration, and DNS Enumeration.

3. What is User Enumeration? Answer: User Enumeration is a type of enumeration technique used to identify valid usernames or user accounts on a target system or network.

4. What is Network Enumeration? Answer: Network Enumeration is a type of enumeration technique used to identify network resources such as IP addresses, open ports, and running services on a target system or network.

5. What is OS Enumeration? Answer: OS Enumeration is a type of enumeration technique used to identify the operating system used by a target system or network.

6. What is Service Enumeration? Answer: Service Enumeration is a type of enumeration technique used to identify the services and applications running on a target system or network.

7. What is File and Share Enumeration? Answer: File and Share Enumeration is a type of enumeration technique used to identify files and shares that are accessible on a target system or network.

8. What is LDAP Enumeration? Answer: LDAP Enumeration is a type of enumeration technique used to identify user and group accounts within an LDAP directory.

9. What is DNS Enumeration? Answer: DNS Enumeration is a type of enumeration technique used to identify domain names and their associated IP addresses.

10. Why is enumeration important in cybersecurity? Answer: Enumeration is important in cybersecurity because it helps identify potential vulnerabilities and attack vectors that can be exploited by attackers. Understanding the different types of enumeration techniques can help security professionals take steps to protect their systems and networks from these types of attacks.

NetBIOS Enumeration Quiz Solutions

1. What is NetBIOS enumeration? Answer: NetBIOS enumeration is the process of collecting information about NetBIOS services running on a target system or network, such as share names, user accounts, and system names.
2. Why is NetBIOS enumeration considered a security risk? Answer: NetBIOS enumeration is considered a security risk because it can reveal information that can be used by attackers to gain unauthorized access to systems or networks.
3. What are some tools used for NetBIOS enumeration? Answer: Some tools used for NetBIOS enumeration include NBTScan, NetBIOS Enumerator, and SoftPerfect Network Scanner.
4. What are some common vulnerabilities that can be identified through NetBIOS enumeration? Answer: Common vulnerabilities that can be identified through NetBIOS enumeration include weak passwords, misconfigured shares, unpatched systems, open ports, missing security updates, and weak encryption.
5. How can organizations protect against NetBIOS enumeration? Answer: Organizations can protect against NetBIOS enumeration by disabling NetBIOS, using firewalls, implementing access controls, using encryption, and conducting regular security assessments.
6. What is the difference between NetBIOS and NetBIOS over TCP/IP? Answer: NetBIOS is a protocol used for communicating with other devices on a network, while NetBIOS over TCP/IP is a variant of NetBIOS that is used over TCP/IP networks.
7. What is the purpose of the NetBIOS name service (NBNS)? Answer: The

purpose of the NBNS is to provide a way for NetBIOS names to be resolved to IP addresses on a network.

8. What are some NetBIOS ports that are commonly used? Answer: Some NetBIOS ports that are commonly used include UDP port 137 (NetBIOS name service), UDP port 138 (NetBIOS datagram service), and TCP port 139 (NetBIOS session service).

9. What is the difference between NetBIOS and SMB? Answer: NetBIOS is a protocol used for communicating with other devices on a network, while SMB (Server Message Block) is a protocol used for sharing files, printers, and other resources on a network.

10. What is the potential impact of a successful NetBIOS enumeration attack? Answer: The potential impact of a successful NetBIOS enumeration attack can range from unauthorized access to sensitive data and resources, to the compromise of entire networks or systems.

SNMP Enumeration Quiz Solutions

1. What is SNMP Enumeration? Answer: SNMP Enumeration is the process of gathering information about SNMP-enabled devices on a network, such as their configuration settings, operating system details, and network interface information.
2. What are the tools used for SNMP Enumeration? Answer: Some tools used for SNMP Enumeration include SNMPWalk, SNMPUtil, SolarWinds Network Performance Monitor, Paessler PRTG Network Monitor, and Net-SNMP.
3. What is SNMPWalk and how is it used? Answer: SNMPWalk is a command-line tool that is used to retrieve SNMP information from devices. It can be used to retrieve a complete SNMP tree from a device.
4. What is SNMPUtil and how is it used? Answer: SNMPUtil is a command-line tool that is used to perform SNMP operations on devices. It can be used to retrieve SNMP information, as well as to set SNMP values.
5. What is SolarWinds Network Performance Monitor and how is it used for SNMP Enumeration? Answer: SolarWinds Network Performance Monitor is a network monitoring tool that includes SNMP Enumeration capabilities. It can be used to monitor SNMP-enabled devices and gather information about their configuration.
6. What is Paessler PRTG Network Monitor and how is it used for SNMP Enumeration? Answer: Paessler PRTG Network Monitor is a network monitoring tool that includes SNMP Enumeration capabilities. It can be used to monitor SNMP-enabled devices and gather information about their configuration.
7. What is Net-SNMP and how is it used for SNMP Enumeration? Answer:

Net-SNMP is a suite of SNMP tools that includes a command-line tool for querying SNMP-enabled devices and retrieving information about their configuration.

8. What are the vulnerabilities that can be identified through SNMP Enumeration? Answer: The vulnerabilities that can be identified through SNMP Enumeration include weak SNMP community strings, SNMP version vulnerabilities, unauthorized access, configuration vulnerabilities, and device vulnerabilities.

9. What are the countermeasures that can be implemented to protect against SNMP Enumeration? Answer: The countermeasures that can be implemented to protect against SNMP Enumeration include strong SNMP community strings, SNMP version control, access controls, encryption, configuration management, and network monitoring.

10. Why is it important to secure SNMP-enabled devices? Answer: It is important to secure SNMP-enabled devices because they can be vulnerable to attacks if they are not properly secured. Attackers can use SNMP Enumeration to gather information about a device's configuration and use that information to launch further attacks.

LDAP Enumeration Quiz Solutions

1. What is LDAP Enumeration? Answer: LDAP Enumeration is the process of gathering information about a target system or network by querying its Lightweight Directory Access Protocol (LDAP) directory service.

2. What are the tools used for LDAP Enumeration? Answer: Some of the tools used for LDAP Enumeration include ldapsearch, JXplorer, enum4linux, and Metasploit.

3. What are the vulnerabilities identified through LDAP Enumeration? Answer: Vulnerabilities identified through LDAP Enumeration include user enumeration, group enumeration, password policy enumeration, share and resource enumeration, and server enumeration.

4. How can LDAP Enumeration be used by attackers? Answer: Attackers can use LDAP Enumeration to gather information about a target system or network that can be used to launch further attacks such as brute force attacks, password spraying, or privilege escalation attacks.

5. What are the countermeasures for LDAP Enumeration? Answer: Counter-measures for LDAP Enumeration include implementing access controls, rate limiting, secure authentication, disabling anonymous LDAP access, implementing network segmentation, monitoring LDAP traffic, implementing password policies, and keeping software up-to-date.

6. What is ldapsearch and how is it used for LDAP Enumeration? Answer: ldapsearch is a command-line tool used for querying LDAP directories. It can be used for LDAP Enumeration by specifying search criteria and performing queries on a target system or network.

7. What is JXplorer and how is it used for LDAP Enumeration? Answer: JX-plorer is a graphical tool used for browsing and querying LDAP directories.

It can be used for LDAP Enumeration by connecting to a target system or network and performing queries to gather information.

8. What is enum4linux and how is it used for LDAP Enumeration? Answer: enum4linux is a tool used for enumerating information from Windows and Samba systems. It includes LDAP Enumeration capabilities that can be used to gather information about LDAP directories.

9. What is Metasploit and how is it used for LDAP Enumeration? Answer: Metasploit is a penetration testing framework that includes modules for LDAP Enumeration. It can be used to scan for LDAP services, perform queries, and gather information about a target system or network.

10. Why is LDAP Enumeration important in cybersecurity? Answer: LDAP Enumeration is important in cybersecurity because it can help identify potential vulnerabilities and attack vectors that can be exploited by attackers. Understanding the techniques and tools used for LDAP Enumeration can help security professionals take steps to protect their systems and networks from these types of attacks.

NTP and NFS Enumeration Quiz Solutions

1. What is NTP Enumeration? Answer: NTP Enumeration is the process of gathering information about NTP (Network Time Protocol) servers on a target system or network, including server IP addresses, versions, and configurations.

2. What is NFS Enumeration? Answer: NFS Enumeration is the process of gathering information about NFS (Network File System) servers on a target system or network, including file systems, permissions, and access controls.

3. What are some tools used for NTP Enumeration? Answer: Some tools used for NTP Enumeration include Nmap, ntpq, and sntp.

4. What are some tools used for NFS Enumeration? Answer: Some tools used for NFS Enumeration include showmount, nfsstat, and Nmap.

5. What are some vulnerabilities that can be identified through NTP and NFS Enumeration? Answer: Vulnerabilities that can be identified through NTP and NFS Enumeration include unauthorized access, weak authentication, denial-of-service attacks, data tampering, and information disclosure.

6. How can organizations prevent unauthorized access to NFS file systems? Answer: Organizations can prevent unauthorized access to NFS file systems by configuring them with appropriate permissions and access controls, and implementing secure authentication mechanisms like NFSv4 or Kerberos.

7. How can organizations prevent NTP-based denial-of-service attacks? Answer: Organizations can prevent NTP-based denial-of-service attacks by implementing firewall rules to block NTP traffic from unauthorized sources and limiting the number of NTP queries allowed from each

source.

8. What is the role of encryption in securing NTP and NFS communications? Answer: Encryption plays an important role in securing NTP and NFS communications by protecting data transmitted over the network. TLS and SSL are commonly used encryption protocols.

9. How often should organizations perform vulnerability assessments for NTP and NFS Enumeration? Answer: Organizations should perform vulnerability assessments for NTP and NFS Enumeration on a regular basis to identify vulnerabilities and address them before they can be exploited by attackers.

10. What are some recommended countermeasures for NTP and NFS Enumeration vulnerabilities? Answer: Recommended countermeasures for NTP and NFS Enumeration vulnerabilities include implementing strong authentication mechanisms, patching vulnerabilities, monitoring network traffic, and regularly performing vulnerability assessments.

SMTP and DNS Enumeration Quiz Solutions

1. What is SMTP Enumeration? Answer: SMTP Enumeration is the process of identifying email addresses associated with a target system or network by querying the Simple Mail Transfer Protocol (SMTP) server.

2. What is DNS Enumeration? Answer: DNS Enumeration is the process of querying the Domain Name System (DNS) to gather information about a target system or network, such as IP addresses, domain names, and subdomains.

3. What are some tools used for SMTP Enumeration? Answer: Some tools used for SMTP Enumeration include smtp-user-enum, smtpscan, and Nmap.

4. What are some tools used for DNS Enumeration? Answer: Some tools used for DNS Enumeration include Nmap, nslookup, and dig.

5. What vulnerabilities can be identified through SMTP Enumeration? Answer: SMTP Enumeration can identify vulnerabilities such as open relays, outdated software, and information leakage.

6. What vulnerabilities can be identified through DNS Enumeration? Answer: DNS Enumeration can identify vulnerabilities such as misconfigured DNS records, outdated software, and information leakage.

7. What countermeasures can be implemented to protect against SMTP Enumeration? Answer: Countermeasures to protect against SMTP Enumeration include restricting access, implementing rate limiting, and disabling open relays.

8. What countermeasures can be implemented to protect against DNS

Enumeration? Answer: Countermeasures to protect against DNS Enumeration include monitoring DNS records, keeping software up to date, and implementing network segmentation.

9. Why is SMTP and DNS Enumeration important in cybersecurity? Answer: SMTP and DNS Enumeration can help identify potential vulnerabilities and attack vectors that can be exploited by attackers. Understanding the different types of Enumeration techniques can help security professionals take steps to protect their systems and networks from these types of attacks.

10. What are some best practices for securing SMTP and DNS servers? Answer: Best practices for securing SMTP and DNS servers include using strong passwords, implementing multi-factor authentication, keeping software up to date with security patches, and hiding the software version of servers to prevent attackers from identifying known vulnerabilities.

Other Enumeration Techniques Quiz Solutions

1. What is IPsec Enumeration? Answer: IPsec Enumeration is the process of identifying IPsec security associations (SAs) between two endpoints, which can be used to exploit vulnerabilities and launch attacks against the network.

2. What is VoIP Enumeration? Answer: VoIP Enumeration is the process of identifying and mapping VoIP devices, such as phones and servers, on a network to gather information that can be used to exploit vulnerabilities and launch attacks against the network.

3. What is RPC Enumeration? Answer: RPC Enumeration is the process of identifying and mapping Remote Procedure Call (RPC) services and applications on a network to gather information that can be used to exploit vulnerabilities and launch attacks against the network.

4. What is Unix/Linux Enumeration? Answer: Unix/Linux Enumeration is the process of identifying and mapping Unix/Linux-based systems and services on a network to gather information that can be used to exploit vulnerabilities and launch attacks against the network.

5. What is Telnet Enumeration? Answer: Telnet Enumeration is the process of identifying and mapping Telnet services on a network to gather information that can be used to exploit vulnerabilities and launch attacks against the network.

6. What is FTP Enumeration? Answer: FTP Enumeration is the process of identifying and mapping File Transfer Protocol (FTP) services on a network to gather information that can be used to exploit vulnerabilities

and launch attacks against the network.

7. What is TFTP Enumeration? Answer: TFTP Enumeration is the process of identifying and mapping Trivial File Transfer Protocol (TFTP) services on a network to gather information that can be used to exploit vulnerabilities and launch attacks against the network.

8. What is SMB Enumeration? Answer: SMB Enumeration is the process of identifying and mapping Server Message Block (SMB) services on a network to gather information that can be used to exploit vulnerabilities and launch attacks against the network.

9. What is IPv6 Enumeration? Answer: IPv6 Enumeration is the process of identifying and mapping IPv6-based systems and services on a network to gather information that can be used to exploit vulnerabilities and launch attacks against the network.

10. What is BGP Enumeration? Answer: BGP Enumeration is the process of identifying and mapping Border Gateway Protocol (BGP) services on a network to gather information that can be used to exploit vulnerabilities and launch attacks against the network.

Enumeration Countermeasures Quiz Solutions

1. What are some general countermeasures to prevent Enumeration attacks? Answer: General countermeasures to prevent Enumeration attacks include implementing strong authentication measures, limiting access to sensitive information, regularly updating and patching systems, and implementing firewalls and intrusion detection systems.

2. How can user enumeration be prevented? Answer: User enumeration can be prevented by implementing strong password policies, using account lockout policies, and limiting the amount of information provided in error messages.

3. What can be done to prevent network enumeration? Answer: Network enumeration can be prevented by implementing secure network configurations, using firewalls, and regularly scanning and monitoring network activity.

4. How can OS enumeration be mitigated? Answer: OS enumeration can be mitigated by implementing secure OS configurations, regularly updating and patching systems, and implementing firewalls and intrusion detection systems.

5. What countermeasures can be used to prevent service enumeration? Answer: Countermeasures to prevent service enumeration include disabling unnecessary services, using secure service configurations, and regularly monitoring and updating services.

6. How can file and share enumeration be prevented? Answer: File and share enumeration can be prevented by using secure file and share configura-

tions, regularly monitoring and updating file and share permissions, and implementing firewalls and intrusion detection systems.

7. What can be done to prevent LDAP enumeration? Answer: LDAP enumeration can be prevented by implementing secure LDAP configurations, using firewalls, and regularly monitoring and updating LDAP permissions.

8. How can DNS enumeration be mitigated? Answer: DNS enumeration can be mitigated by implementing secure DNS configurations, regularly monitoring and updating DNS records, and using firewalls.

9. What are some countermeasures to prevent NTP and NFS enumeration? Answer: Countermeasures to prevent NTP and NFS enumeration include implementing secure configurations, using firewalls and intrusion detection systems, and regularly monitoring and updating systems.

10. How can SMTP and DNS enumeration be prevented? Answer: SMTP and DNS enumeration can be prevented by implementing secure configurations, using firewalls and intrusion detection systems, and regularly monitoring and updating systems. Additionally, using strong authentication measures can prevent unauthorized access to sensitive information.